Take Charge!

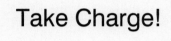

Greg Bustin

TAKE
CHARGE

How Leaders Profit From Change.

TAPESTRY PRESS
IRVING, TEXAS

Tapestry Press
3649 Conflans Road
Suite 103
Irving, TX 75061

Printed in the U.S.A.
08 07 06 05 04   1 2 3 4 5

Library of Congress Cataloging-in-Publication Data
Bustin, Gregory Marlowe, 1955-
   Take charge! : how leaders profit from change / Greg Bustin.
      p. cm.
   Includes bibliographical references and index.
   ISBN 1-930819-35-8 (trade paper : alk. paper) -- ISBN 1-930819-39-0 (hard
cover : alk. paper)
   1. Organizational change. 2. Executive ability. 3. Leadership. I. Title.
   HD58.8.B9 2004
   658.4'092--dc22

                                         2004018175

Book design and layout by
D. & F. Scott Publishing, Inc.
N. Richland Hills, Texas

Cover by Eisenberg & Associates
Dallas, Texas

"The world is too big for us. Too much is going on, too many crimes, too much violence and excitement. Try as you will, you get behind in the race in spite of yourself. It is an incessant strain to keep pace, and still you lose ground. Science empties its discoveries on you so fast you stagger beneath them in hopeless bewilderment. The political world is now changing so rapidly that you're out of breath trying to keep pace with who's in and who's out. Everything is high pressure. Human nature can't endure much more."

—From *The Atlantic Journal*, June 16, 1833

Plus c' change, plus c'est la même chose.

(The more things change, the more they are the same.)

—From *Les Guêpes* by Alphonse Karr, December 1839

To my parents,
John and Roselyn,
for pointing the way,
and to Janet and Jordan
for their love and support.

Contents

Introduction

On the night before my wife and I left on vacation many years ago, I got the news: I would become the general manager of the company shortly after my return.

My boss had taken the top post at a New York firm, and in a matter of weeks, the business she had salvaged from debt and thrust into profitability would be in my hands. The colleagues she was nurturing into professionals would be my charges. And the seasoned veteran who had been my mentor for the last five years would be my competitor. I was 32 years old.

Nothing kills a vacation like visceral fear.

Have you suddenly found yourself in charge? Or if you've been in charge for some time, has the prospect of a close-in victory prompted you to consider new actions to accelerate success? Perhaps the possibility of a failure is looming large and, in your role as the leader, all eyes and ears are trained on you to learn what must be done to prevent a catastrophe.

At the time of my first hot-seat experience seventeen years ago, I had the words "What if . . ." framed and hung on my wall. Those words reminded me that a creative mind is a questioning mind. But in my early days as the top leader of my business unit, those two questioning words became the semantic launching pad for many a gloomy scenario.

I tackled the issues associated with this change and came out on top. During this encounter and others like it, I grew to appreciate the opportunities change presents leaders. In 1994, I founded my own consulting firm. Years later, after dissecting the hundreds of engagements our firm has completed, it's clear these engagements are all rooted in change. It can be the kind of change that's an outgrowth of positive developments, such as fast growth, launching a new product or service, the need to expand sales territory, or a new leader ascending to the head of an organization. Just as often, our clients have needed us to help them to respond to change brought on by problems, such as declining sales, new regulatory restrictions, the process of reorganization under bankruptcy protection or, worst of all, a fatality in which their business was implicated.

Our clients' greatest successes occur when we collaborate with leaders who are committed to making substantive changes to correct or capitalize on the changes their own organizations are facing. These leaders really want to implement new programs, not just talk about them or say why something bold can't be done. These men and women champ at the bit to build on their success and can hardly wait to get started each day to examine ways to test or pursue a new opportunity. In other cases, the pain felt by executives has passed a final threshold that prompts them at last to break the bonds of inertia and take meaningful, corrective action so their organization can resolve the problem and move on.

Change—and the opportunity for change—is all around us. It seems as if there's been a lot more change occurring lately. Maybe so. Perhaps the stakes are a bit higher. But change has been with us since the dawn of humankind and it's here to stay. Change is inevitable.

Leaders wrestle with change on a regular basis. Isn't this what you're facing? Whether it's enterprise-wide, bet-your-business, transformational change or incremental adjustments concerning a particular person, product, or operational component, change is everywhere.

So it struck me that the problems, opportunities, questions, and doubts arising from change demand resolutions that transcend "smart answers." Leveraging change requires the intellectual, emotional, spiritual grounding, and guts to make and implement tough choices. It means bringing to light timeless principles over and over again and then implementing them. Looking at those age-old principles for tackling change helped me to fully appreciate the old saying: the more things change, the more they really do stay the same.

This book was written from the front lines of business to serve as a guide for leaders whose organizations are experiencing change—whether change comes at you from the pot-of-gold end of the rainbow, or from the septic tank end. It combines into a single volume the best aspects of historical perspective, relevant cases, practical steps, and inspirational points of view from leaders who have wrestled with change and come out on top, including my own first-hand experiences. It examines leaders who have ignored fundamentals and paid for it with their jobs or the demise of the companies they managed.

This book is for any leader who wants to:

- Identify and better understand the dynamics of change within their organization and in the world around them.
- Learn and profit from the timeless principles and proven fundamentals that other leaders—kings and queens, politicians and athletes, business executives and generals—have brought to bear in their successful encounters with change.
- Acquire specific guidelines that can be implemented to undertake and measure new strategies, procedures, and initiatives to leverage change for his or her advantage.
- Begin to think in different ways, approaching old problems from fresh perspectives in order to change their organization for the better.

And though you'll find plenty of anecdotes, real world examples and practical suggestions between the covers, this book is less about checklists and more about helping you examine your appetite for change and your intentions for approaching the change that is occurring—or that needs to occur—in your organization.

You'll also find cartoons that correspond to the topics being addressed throughout this book since I believe humor is a quality vital to those leading their organizations through change and uncertainty. The best leaders take time to laugh, and exceptional leaders laugh loudest at themselves.

We will lead you from general principles for responding to change to increasingly detailed strategies for coping with specific situations. Part 1 addresses the implications of change that leaders face in every organization. Part 2 describes the personal and professional characteristics leaders must develop and cultivate to harness the power of change. Part 3 articulates the universal principles for preparing organizations to succeed in changing environments. Part 4 provides tools and guidelines for companies to achieve a competitive advantage in times of change and uncertainty. Part 5 discusses strategies for shaking up complacent organizations. Part 6 identifies organizational distress signals and the steps required to achieve positive outcomes. Part 7 recommends approaches for keeping an organization on track as it capitalizes on change.

It's up to you to take charge and profit from change.

Part 1

You're in Charge—Now What?

"O.K.! Time to make a wish, clear it with me, and blow out the candles."

1

What It Means to Lead in Times of Change

You've moved into the executive office; your employees await your instructions. You face a thousand possible courses of action. Where do you start?

Begin by considering three guiding principles about leading in times of change.

First, great leaders don't micromanage. The difference between a leader and a manager is, to paraphrase Mark Twain, the difference between lightning and the lightning bug.

A manager tells someone what to do. And a micromanager not only tells someone what to do but how to do it, and may ask for updates on the hour or by the day. As a leader, you must avoid this trap. Otherwise, the ability of your organization to grow and flourish during changing times will be directly proportional to how much work you can personally oversee. Further, talented staff responds to a supervisor's lack of trust not by working harder but by becoming frustrated and eventually departing. This results in a perpetual revolving door that will drain time, focus, and energy from those up and down the chain of command, developments that are particularly distracting and counterproductive during times of change. "The best executive," said President Theodore Roosevelt, "is the one who has sense enough to pick good men to do what he wants done, and self-restraint

7

enough to keep from meddling with them while they do it." In other words, great leaders hire the best then break down barriers, freeing those working for them to do their best. Exceptional leaders then get out of the way.

Second, great leaders define success on their own terms. They must be willing to buck trends, question premises, and try new approaches—all critical qualities in times of change and uncertainty. Great leaders are the first to admit mistakes and the last to give up. They're not always popular, though a good leader is always respected. They're not necessarily famous or even charismatic, but they motivate their employees to get the job done at consistently high levels of performance. If this approach defines your leadership style, you can expect those in your organization to agree with the ancient Arab proverb that says, "On the day of victory, no one is tired."

Third, great leaders operate from sound principles. No matter how much more complex the world of business seems to get and no matter how much more quickly we race to outrun the competition, great leaders *always* operate from a set of guiding principles that haven't changed much over the centuries. So you must be willing to back your principles with courage and action. Alexander Hamilton noted that, "The manner in which a thing is done has more influence than is commonly imagined."

The success of any organization—particularly in times of change—depends on a great leader who is:

- The literal and figurative embodiment of an organization
- Responsible for setting the strategy and holding the moral compass of an enterprise
- Accountable for delivering on promises
- Blessed with the beliefs, position and resources to turn crises into victories
- The final arbiter on aligning values with actions

And to paraphrase President Harry S.Truman, a leader is where the buck is supposed to stop.

In times of change, it's up to you to take charge.

"*Let's just say that I've lived up to the highest moral code permitted by law.*"

2

A Fragile Trust

More than ever, effective leadership requires integrity. "A good reputation is more valuable than money," Publius Syrus said twenty-one hundred years ago. Odd that some might consider this thinking an old-fashioned, outdated notion. But Warren Buffett of Berkshire Hathaway provides an updated view of the importance of reputation by telling his managers that "We can afford to lose money—even a lot of money. We cannot afford to lose reputation—even a shred of reputation."[1]

In our brand-conscious society, an organization's leader is an extension of its image, especially in changing times. Flux and uncertainty provide more opportunities—some might say pitfalls—for tough decision-making. Nevertheless, your organization, its stakeholders, and the public expect you to act with integrity.

But get ready for what you're up against. Nearly two-thirds of Americans hold the top leaders personally responsible for restoring trust and confidence in American business, one study found,[2] while another identified unethical behavior and media criticism as the highest threats to a company's reputation.[3] The lack of integrity being demonstrated over the last few years by so-called leaders has been truly frightening. Poor ethical judgment will do what even a shaky economy cannot: topple the mighty.

Unfortunately, some of today's bad behavior comes from fundamentally flawed executives being chosen to run companies. "Chainsaw" Al Dunlap, for instance, had a history of questionable business practices dating back twenty years—long before his misdeeds at Sunbeam brought him down. Dennis Kozlowski, who was removed at Tyco following charges of financially criminal acts, misrepresented his own achievements as early as 1988.[4] Small untruths make it easier to tell larger lies the next time. The man who's cheating on his test today may be cheating the SEC tomorrow. The woman who promotes herself beyond her abilities may next be trumpeting attributes that a product doesn't have. Tigers don't change their stripes.

Integrity goes beyond technical compliance with the law. As head of the New York Stock Exchange, Richard Grasso accepted a $140 million payday that had been approved by the board and written into his contract. But at a time when reformers rightfully had the NYSE under the microscope, the appearance of conflicts, the hint of preferred treatment and compensation perceived as "destructive . . . of fairness"[5] prompted Grasso to resign one hundred days after the news about his contract (and huge paycheck) was made public. "The role of the NYSE is to curb excesses," said one executive whose institutional funds are invested in NYSE stocks. "How can you pay someone $11 million a year to do this?"[6]

The net effect of difficult circumstances—including chief executives' sins of commission and omission—adds up to an even tougher challenge for leading during changing times. Reputation can affect the bottom line. Indeed, research shows that "a 10% change in CEO reputation is estimated to result in a 24% change in a company's market capitalization."[7] As a result, chief executive reputation affects chief executive tenure. "A decade ago," reports *The New York Times*, "if a big institutional shareholder like a pension or mutual fund did not like management, it sold the stock. Now it presses the board to drop the chief executive."[8] As a result, chief executives can expect to spend three years in their position, down from 9.5 years in 1995, according to various studies,[9] and one report estimated that fully one-quarter of America's largest companies named a new chief executive in 2003.[10]

Even more troubling is a report released showing that only 54 percent of Americans working in the private sector believe most corporate executives are honest and ethical.[11]

Some chief executives, at least, seem to be getting the message that they are responsible for the welfare and management of their organization's reputation. Indeed, one study reported that 65 percent of chief executives surveyed said reputation is their job, versus 14 percent who said reputation was the responsibility of the board, and 12 percent who said reputation management was the responsibility of the communications department.[12] While these findings are encouraging, this study nevertheless suggests that some executives still do not factor into their vision of leadership President Truman's "the buck stops here" approach to personal responsibility.

Yet through the years, leaders have followed five guidelines that help them do the right thing:

1. Admit You're Capable of Straying from the Ethical Path

It's healthy to realize that you're capable of making an unethical decision. It's true that there is some bad in the best person and some good in the worst. Or as a Chinese proverb says, "There are two perfect men—one dead, the other unborn." Stay vigilant.

2. Calibrate Your Own Moral Compass

Whether you take guidance from Aristotle, the Bible, or Stephen Covey, you'll find that the important philosophers, the major world religions, and all corporate mission statements distill the essence of success to the timeless qualities of honesty, fairness, respect, and service. "I do without being commanded," Aristotle said, "what others do only from fear of the law."

3. Gather People with Courage

Find and keep people around you—inside and outside your company—that have the courage to disagree with you on logical and ethical grounds. It's been said that if two people agree on everything all the time, one of them is superfluous. Yes-men and -women don't add value to your decisions.

4. Right and Wrong Are Clearly Delineated in Most Cases

A good rule of thumb is that if it takes more than thirty seconds to weigh the alternatives and determine if an opportunity is morally, not just technically, right, then it's probably morally wrong, and you need to pass on that opportunity. As humans we can rationalize anything. So check your motives. Don't tempt yourself. Never allow circumstances to affect your ability to make ethical decisions.

5. Communicate Successes and Mistakes Honestly

Obscuring the truth does not pay. But there have been many instances when making a tough, right decision has built leaders and leading companies, and we'll examine several later in this book. In those instances where an apology is called for, make sure it's genuine. We've all seen cases where the apology is recited in an insincere manner as a public-relations ploy.

● ● ●

Integrity transcends the moment. Consider the Native American belief in the power and righteousness of multigenerational thinking. The idea is simple, but the execution is difficult: Every decision you make must withstand seven generations previous and seven generations hence. Each generation must be rooted in the experience of the past and be able to weather the scrutiny of the future. In today's instant-gratification society, such thinking may sound quaint. But I first heard this concept expressed in 1993 by the chief executive of Mary Kay Cosmetics, a company founded in 1963 by a woman with vision and principles. The company's revenue for 2003 exceeded 2002's record of $1.6 billion wholesale.[13]

When you're in the trenches battling change, it can be difficult to act with integrity and to think down the road. But time has a way of clarifying right and wrong. History is full of men and women who would like to rethink some of their moral predicaments, and the last few years have, unfortunately, added more names to this list. History also records those who acted heroically. We'll examine more of both in chapter 7.

C.E.O. OF THE MONTH

3

Your First (or Next) 100 Days as the Chief

You're in charge. The ultimate responsibility for the success or failure of your organization is in your hands. People are counting on you to help them succeed.

Maybe you've been promoted to a new level of responsibility within your organization. Perhaps you've recently moved into a leadership position at a company that's expecting you to be a change agent. Or maybe as the top leader for some time, the situation in which you now find yourself has prompted you to take action and chart a new course for success.

Whether you're looking at your first one hundred days in a new position or the next one hundred days as part of a freshly acquired sense of urgency, remember that smart, focused, decisive action that's grounded in integrity is the only way to effect positive change.

Here are seven proven steps to take in the first days and weeks of finding yourself face to face with change:

1. Set a New Objective, and Redefine the Status Quo

When faced with major change, your first instinct cannot be to proceed with "business as usual" in the hope that your past record will ensure your future success. It's a logical line of reasoning, but it just doesn't work. This is especially true if the change you face resulted from problems associated with your predecessor—be they ethical, operational or financial. If you've been in your position for some time, ask yourself, "What would new

17

management do if they were to come in and replace the existing team?" Well, what's holding you back? Establish a new set of measurable objectives, chart your course, and make the changes you know in your gut must be made. You must call into question every policy, every system, every operating procedure. Do your best to separate fact from fiction, valued traditions from counter-productive habits. Develop your plan, and act. Do it your way. After all, you'll be the one taking the heat if things go south.

2. Prepare for the Worst

Think things through and log every worst-case scenario you can think of—especially the ones that shake you in the middle of the night. *How will you respond to certain events? What's your contingency plan if your first plan fails? What unexpected event could occur?* You may consider this approach overly fretful and counterproductive. But consider former Intel Chief Executive Andy Grove's philosophy: "Only the paranoid survive." Keep worrying—this is part of your job. This is not to say you can't have fun, but leaders must expect the unexpected. "A general-in-chief," said Napoleon, "should ask himself frequently in the day, 'What would I do if the enemy's army appeared now in my front, or on my right, or on my left?' If he has any difficulty in answering these questions, his position is bad, and he should seek to remedy it."[14] Armed with your questions and scenarios, quiz your outgoing superior, whether you're the beneficiary of an orderly transition or a "palace coup." Even if you choose to not follow their advice, you'll be glad to have secured their final perspective.

3. Be Honest with Employees

Any change at the top necessarily reshapes your corporate culture, and your employees will be watching to see what's different, as well they should. Whether they articulate them or not, your employees have questions, and you must address them candidly. It's up to you to communicate your one-hundred-day plan and your expectations. Robert E. Lee called duty "the most sublime word in the English language," and your job as the new (or newly in-spired) commander must be to tell employees theirs. It may sound paradoxical, but duty provides a sense of freedom for employees because it frees them from making bad choices. Tell your employees what you expect, and explain any new ground rules or code of conduct under which the organization will operate. Now is not the time to sugarcoat things. Inform your people of the challenges you face as an organization, and their pivotal role in overcoming them. Finally, make clear the rewards and consequences of acceptable and unacceptable performance.

4. Meet with Customers

It's possible that your business represents or works with a number of organizations that you know little about. Schedule get-acquainted meetings with every major client, partner, and supplier, and bring yourself up to speed on their special requirements in a hurry. If you've been in your position for some time, meet with clients, partners, and suppliers again, this time listening to what they're telling you through the filter of change. Dan Edelman—founder and chairman of Edelman Worldwide, the world's largest independent public relations firm and sixth largest overall—still flies around the world meeting with clients, and he always asks them three simple but powerful questions:

- How's your business?
- How are we performing for you?
- What else can we help you with?

Such meetings with clients, for example, are more than perfunctory. They signify a genuine interest in their companies and your unflagging desire for their business. So use these meetings to recommit to serving your customers well, or to commit to addressing problems. Then make sure you fix things you say you're going to fix.

5. Delegate

Although you must master key information, avoid immersing yourself in so much detail that you feel like you have two or three jobs. This experience can be like spinning china plates on sticks: the longer you keep it up, the greater the odds of a crash. Lightening your load is the only recourse. Take a good look at your workload, size up your lieutenants, and give them all they can handle. You're not dumping on them so much as sharing the opportunity for learning and growth. World War II British general Bernard Montgomery said a leader must have "the capacity and the will to rally men and women to a common purpose and the character which will inspire confidence."[15] When you inspire your troops and delegate effectively, you'll bring them with you up the ladder to new challenges and opportunities.

6. Reward Effective Employees

Leaders must back up promises with tangible evidence. Recognize new levels of leadership with raises and promotions. After I was promoted into my first overall management role, I awarded more raises and promotions to my team members based on their performance than at any single time in the history of our business unit. You'll find the money is merely a symbol of the confidence and value you have placed in your employees. The true motivator for them is the spirit of cooperation that comes with a shared vision. However, those employees that can't step up must be asked to step aside. Failure to weed out underperformers sends the wrong signal to those who have embraced your new challenges and hinders your ability to effect positive change.

7. Create a SWAT Team of Experts

Reach out to people outside your organization for counsel: your lawyer and CPA, outside consultants, close friends, peers in other organizations that you admire. You may not be familiar with other areas of your organization's operations. If that's the case, take a crash course in all areas of in-house operations—accounting, IT, production, marketing, sales—and build alliances with key supervisors in the process. Make sure you and your banker see eye-to-eye. Throughout this process, you're looking for a few trusted advisors you can count on to shoot straight with you.

● ● ●

Redefining the status quo is probably the most exhilarating challenge you'll face when you take charge of an organization. For better or worse, it will be remade in your image.

Part 2

Preparing Yourself for Change

"Relax, honey—change is good."

4

Change
Problem or Opportunity?

Your ability (or inability) to capitalize on change is rooted in how you view it. If you view change as an alteration or an occurrence where people and organizations take on new forms, you're right, of course. In this instance, you're viewing change as a noun—a condition to be managed, tolerated, and, ultimately, adjusted to. You may even go so far as to say that change is a problem. It's a bucking bronco that can be difficult to corral, tame, and ride.

If, on the other hand, you consider change an action word that means the lively activity of transforming a person, object, opportunity, or organization, then you've grasped the essence of what is required to lead during changing times. And it is this: If you do not seize the opportunities presented by changes inside and outside your organization to control your own destiny and cause positive change to occur, someone else will.

You may be feeling that you're swept up in waves of change that pound you relentlessly. As a result, you're probably reexamining business practices more often than ever before. You're continually seeking, identifying, quantifying, and debating new options. *How do we balance the need for long-term thinking and investment in a market that judges success in 90-day increments? Is our competitive advantage sustainable? Who are our best customers? Who are our best employees? Will one stumble erode the trust we've spent a corporate lifetime earning? How do we effectively address the tension between prag-matism and idealism?*

We'll tackle these questions in upcoming chapters. First, let's make sure you're on board for change.

It can be tempting to say the need to address change is unnecessary. After all, responding to change goes against human nature—most of us are content to stay rooted in the familiar. It's easy to be lulled into believing that the safe bet—the path of least resistance—is the road to winning. This premise can be just as risky as making a change. Don't get me wrong. Not all conservative decisions are bad—only those that breed complacency and status-quo thinking.

It's also easy to argue that choices involving change are not as clear at the time a decision must be made as they are in hindsight.

But these notions and others like them are excuses.

From working with hundreds of leaders to help them profit from change and from observing hundreds more wrestling with change, I know that embracing change and making the right choices—difficult and painful though they may be—will help companies push through tough times to survive and, in some cases, thrive. Likewise, executives shirking the responsibility of making a tough decision or exercising bad judgment will eventually cause an organization to fail—or cost those at the top their jobs. Your choice is to change your practices or perish. You must constantly challenge the status quo.

Change for change's sake is not what I'm talking about. As Dan Scoggin, former chief executive of T.G.I. Friday's, used to tell me and anyone else that was in earshot, "Activity without results is meaningless." And he's right. Changing times don't necessarily require you to reinvent the wheel or overhaul your system, but any sort of change provides an ideal platform to reexamine existing practices and introduce new or improved levels of standards, procedures, and fresh ways of thinking.

Taking charge in changing times requires adopting an attitude that:

- Embraces uncertainty because of the opportunity it presents
- Understands that uncertainty brings a certain fluidity to your life and those you lead
- Moves ahead courageously into the unknown

In the coming chapters we will examine the following three imperatives:

1. Constantly Critique Yourself

What worked before may not work today. Don't become so fixed in your patterns that you forget the original objective. Like the old joke goes, "when you're up to your neck in alligators, it's easy to forget the original objective was to drain the swamp."

2. Stay Alert

You must expect the unexpected as you move toward your potential. You must be intentional. And you must be urgent. "Things may come to those who wait," said Abraham Lincoln, "but only the things left by those who hustle."

3. Motivate Your Organization to Move Together

You must inspire your troops and get them to commit to the mission and to one another. Then you must hold them accountable to one another. Those that aren't committed to change will hold back those who are, and that can be a big problem. As Benjamin Franklin remarked, "We must all hang together, or assuredly we will all hang separately."

● ● ●

Where there is change, there is opportunity for failure or success. You can choose your path.

Know Thyself

5

"Know Thyself"

How do you ground your organization in a set of core values while your strategies and practices adapt to a changing world? How do you define what your organization stands for? How do you create a framework for ethical decision-making and communicate and instill this framework throughout your business so that it becomes second nature? And how do you prepare for and manage through the crises that so often accompany change?

Every organization is different. And the situations their leaders face are different. Yet all successful organizations—and all successful leaders—have a set of guiding principles.

As you've probably already figured out, one of the first steps you must take in answering the tough questions that always arise as a result of change, uncertainty, or adversity is to understand your own beliefs.

To be human is to be a believer. We don't all believe the same thing, and some of us hold beliefs more intensely than others, but we insist in believing in something. It's part of our human condition. Beliefs form the foundation of personal and organizational character as depicted below:

Thoughts → Beliefs → Values → Actions → Habits → Character

Beliefs are not created—they are developed and shaped over time. They are then discovered. Only then can they be codified. The American Declaration of Independence is a stunning example of articulating—not creating—a nation's beliefs. Thomas Jefferson said the document was "neither aiming at originality of principle or sentiment, nor yet copied from any previous writing, it was intended to be an expression of the American mind, and to give that expression the proper tone and spirit called for by the occasion."[16]

Okay, so you're not Jefferson. Who is? But go back in time way past Jefferson before you try to get your organization to go along with you, because you must first come to grips with your own tolerance for change.

- How do you feel about change?
- Are you up for implementing change?
- Do you believe your organization really needs to change?
- How much change is enough?
- What things should we not change?

Start by following the lead of Greek philosopher Socrates, who believed that deep within everything concrete is the idea of the thing itself, or its essence. "Know thyself," Socrates said. He believed that self-knowledge is the starting point because the greatest source of confusion is the failure to realize how little we know about anything, including ourselves.

Fast forward to the 20th century for the perspective of Thomas Watson, Jr., the son of IBM's founder.

"Consider any great organization," wrote Watson in *A Business and Its Beliefs*, "and you will find that it owes its resiliency not to its form of organizational or administrative skills, but to the power of what we call beliefs and the appeals these beliefs have for its people. I firmly believe that any organization, in order to survive and achieve success, must have a sound set of beliefs on which it premises its policies and actions."[17]

Knowing yourself, therefore, means understanding how you'll respond in the pressure-cooker environment that's often created by change. You'll find that your mettle as a leader is not truly tested until your principles are put to the test. This means principles aren't principles until they have the potential to cost you something. Money. Power. Position. Lives. Reputation.

"I'm not trying to change you—I'm trying to enhance you."

6

You Are Here

Take a few minutes to gauge your organization's situation by examining the following twelve statements. Answer True if the statement describes your organization or False if not, then read on for the answers.

1. We've enjoyed success on a consistent basis, so it doesn't make sense to look at changing what we're doing. Why mess with success?

2. All of our senior management team members need to agree with where we are and where we're trying to go before we begin implementing any initiative.

3. I'm more of a detail person than a visionary, so the chances of our organization embracing any type of bold initiative are pretty small.

4. We use an annual planning process to set objectives for each part of our organization and to develop new programs. This is the best way to examine change and to determine whether there are new opportunities to pursue or our existing programs need to be tweaked or terminated.

5. It's important to have 80 percent of the data secured and analyzed before we commit to any new initiative.

6. The press of business has made time one of our most precious commodities. Spending management time on a strate-

gic planning exercise just doesn't seem to make sense for us right now.

7. We're already implementing a plan. Even though the plan is not working as well as we'd like, it's premature to scrap it and start all over. Besides, doing so would be a major disruption to our people, and altering what we're doing would not reflect well on management.

8. I'm not sure how much change our people can handle all at once. The best way to transform our company will be to make small, incremental changes.

9. The problem with coming up with new ideas is that they can be very hard to implement. Whatever goal we set, we had better be able to achieve it.

10. Outside factors in our industry are already creating changes that are challenging our organization. I don't want to create more disruption.

11. I'm always prepared to try new things. If things don't work out the way we hoped, we can always return to the practices we've used in our business in the past.

12. The devil I know is better than the devil I don't know.

Change Is in the Air—Or Is It?

An executive prepared to leverage change would answer as follows:

1. *False.* Too much reliance on even a successful strategy, service, or product can impede innovation and improvement. Consider Campbell's soup. For years, the leaders at Campbell Soup Co. did not fully appreciate the growing demand for healthier and more convenient foods. While the ready-to-serve soups have grown, Merrill Lynch & Co. noted the company's condensed soup business (which is the lion's

share of total US soup sales) has fallen 21 percent since 1998.[18] "Even if you're on the right track, you'll get run over if you just sit there," said Will Rogers. The best never rest.

2. *True.* Lack of alignment among the management team will, at the least, hold back an organization and, at worst, kill it. So if you can't achieve alignment after letting every senior team member know your objectives and your strategies for accomplishing them, it's best to ask those who fundamentally disagree with you to move on. Disagreement among seniors will trickle down through the organization and dilute or even poison daily operations.

3. *False.* You don't need to be a so-called visionary to lead a change initiative. What's important is determining how to make the most of changes facing your organization and then developing a plan that moves your organization from point A to point B. Your attention to detail improves your organization's chances of success, since detail people are comfortable setting clear objectives, building in milestones, and holding people accountable for executing the plan. This is not micromanagement; it's leadership.

4. *True.* Annual planning, when approached with an anything's-possible attitude, can be the logical launching pad for any change initiative. The planning process, used as a framework to entertain new ideas and question old practices, is an effective tool. Don't let planning dissolve into a rote and mindless method of budgeting based on a set of premises that may be incorrect, ineffective, or outdated. Also, don't wait on the calendar to conduct an enterprise-wide planning exercise if you face an immediate opportunity or threat.

5. *False.* Excessive delays in the name of information-gathering avoids decision-making and turns into "analysis paraly-

sis." US Secretary of State Colin Powell uses the formula "P = 40–70, in which P stands for the probability of success . . . Once the information is in the 40 to 70 range, go with your gut."[19] The idea is to delay action if you have only enough information to give you less than a 40 percent chance of being right. But don't wait until you have enough facts to be 100 percent sure, because by then it is almost always too late. Procrastination in the name of reducing risk actually increases risk.

6. *False.* Everyone's busy, so understand that argument for what it is: an excuse to postpone what must be done. A person is defined by the battles they fight and the battles they avoid. Failing to take time to plan—particularly in times of change—is avoiding a battle where the outcome determines tomorrow's victor. Planning provides an opportunity to catch your breath, clear your head, assess your efforts, and adjust your direction away from the heat of the battle. Failure to plan is a plan to fail.

7. *False.* The definition of insanity, it's been said, is doing the same thing over and over and expecting different results. So when things aren't working according to your plans, your challenge as a leader is to know, as the Kenny Rogers song says, "when to hold 'em, and know when to fold 'em." Of course, if you're listening to your customers, watching your competitors, and measuring internal performance, you'll have a clearer picture of which things aren't working and why, and what must be done to improve your situation. By the way, your people will already know things aren't working and will not be surprised if you initiate changes; on the contrary, they will be surprised if you don't.

8. *True.* The longest journey, say the Chinese, begins with the smallest step. So if you believe a little movement in the

right direction will allow your team to become comfortable with change, take those first steps. Particularly in times of trouble, giving people a few simple, concrete tasks gets them engaged, restores productivity, and lifts their spirits. Remember to articulate a destination, supply a road map, and help your team understand that the small steps being taken today are part of a broader, bigger, and better plan for renewed or continued success.

9. *True.* Nothing will sap the energy of a team quicker than getting their hopes up then not following through. "Beware the genius manager," writes Peter Drucker. "Management is doing a very few simple things and doing them well. Most of the time it is hard work to get a very few simple things across so that ordinary people can do it."[20] Don't ignore big ideas, but make sure the little things are getting done.

10. *False.* Face it. Disruption is a given in most industries these days. You can either work to control your own destiny or have your destiny controlled by others. Dell, Wal-Mart, and Southwest Airlines—all operating in chaotic industries with razor-thin margins—rose above the fray by creating their own models for success. You can, too. Don't confuse constant motion, rapid movement, and short-term projects with the need for a long-term strategy for success.

11. *False.* You've heard the expression "burning the boats" to summarize decisiveness and commitment. Ancient Greek commanders torched their ships after landing in a new land to fight an enemy on its home turf. The message to the troops was clear: *We've made our decision. There's no turning back. We're committed to victory.* If your troops sense you're not committed to making changes to achieve your objectives, they'll believe there will always be an opportunity to turn back if the changes don't work. That type of attitude

will kill any commitment to a change initiative before it's
had a chance to succeed.

12. *False*. If your organization finds itself in an unfavorable
     situation, maintaining the status quo by its very defini-
     tion will not improve your position. Failure to put a new
     plan in place in such times is to surrender to defeat, or to
     deny that problems exist, or to hope those problems will
     either somehow improve or simply go away. Surrender
     means giving up, denial is deadly, and "hope," says Chief
     Executive Jim Buchanan of Buchanan Associates, "is not
     a plan." Buchanan should know. He's battled through
     two recessions since founding his technology firm on the
     way toward being recognized a record seven times by the
     Dallas 100, the award program for fast-growing, success-
     ful companies. Knowledge is the only way to conquer
     your fear of the unknown, so figure out what you know,
     what you don't know, and what must be done to improve
     your situation. "When God is planning ruin for a man,"
     goes the ancient proverb, "He first deprives him of his
     reason." In times of difficulty, uncertainty, and change,
     failure to act is an unreasonable decision that can mean
     death to an organization.

● ● ●

If your answers matched eight or more of the answers given
here, then you're up to the challenge that comes with embracing change, and you're ready to use change to your advantage. If your answers matched between five and seven of the
answers given here, you're ambivalent about tackling change.
That's a difficult place for a leader to be because your employees
will have enough anxiety about the uncertainties that accompany change. If you're uncertain, too, it will show, and your
employees' confidence in you and your plans will be under-

mined. And if your answers matched four or fewer of the answers given here, your chances of succeeding in times of change will be small unless you seek and follow advice from others with experience, conviction, and confidence.

"I'm a social scientist, Michael. That means I can't explain electricity or anything like that, but if you ever want to know about people I'm your man."

7

Nine Attributes
You'll Need to Tackle
Change

Now that you've measured your own tolerance for change, let's look at nine attributes of great men and women who can serve as inspirations in your quest to profit from change.

This brief study of great leaders is not intended to be definitive. Rather, we will extract leadership attributes that great leaders have shared across the centuries. A collection of great attributes is not new. Aristotle articulated his twelve "Virtues" twenty-three hundred years ago. *The Rule of St. Benedict* was written around 530 as a guide not only for religious communities, but for any person desiring a more fulfilling life. Benjamin Franklin reflected on "moral perfection" in his thirteen "virtues with their precepts" more than 250 years ago. British general Sir Robert Baden-Powell's Scout Law, codified in 1908, names twelve qualities designed to build and nurture citizenship.

We will focus on nine characteristics shared by leaders who have confronted change and turned it to their advantage. These characteristics are so fundamental, so timeless, that they should be obvious. But just because they're obvious doesn't mean they're easy to adhere to—especially on a consistent basis. Alongside heroes, we'll also look at some reverse role models that failed to apply one or more of these nine fundamentals.

Great leaders are:
- Honest
- Articulate
- Aspirational
- Practical
- Decisive
- Disciplined
- Responsible
- Respectful
- Persistent

Honest

As a guiding principle, honesty tops the list of attributes of all great leaders.

Change brings uncertainty. *Will I lose my job? Is the company relocating? Is the plant closing? Can I do the job? Will this lawsuit kill the company? Can I meet the deadline? Is this new job a real opportunity or is it a way to transition me out of the organization? Is the entire organization behind me on this new initiative?*

People want to know the score so they can make their own decisions. They need the unvarnished truth. They may not like what they're told, but they need to hear the truth, and it's your responsibility to give it to them. Failure to do so can have two unfavorable consequences, both of which are worse than what you may consider the short-term pain of being honest. First, you're simply delaying the inevitable because sooner or later, the truth will emerge. Second, when it does, your credibility will be shot to pieces for not shooting straight in the first place. Executives who lie or even shade the truth cannot expect their organizations to continue to believe in them, much less follow them.

Whether the promise is little or big makes no difference to the person on the receiving end if you don't deliver. When you tell the truth and honor your commitments, you earn someone's trust. But when you don't do what you say you're going to do, you lose it. Few guidelines are as black and white as this one: Always tell the truth.

The absence of truth is also a lie.

That's what brought down Don Carty, chief executive of AMR Corporation, parent of American Airlines. The world's largest airline had been hit hard by both the recession that began in April 2001 and the events of September 11, 2001. Air travel evaporated, and soon, so did the company's cash. By the spring of 2003, its business was in a tailspin, hemorrhaging money at a rate of $10 million each day. Carty wanted desperately to keep American out of bankruptcy. He was making progress, having negotiated $1.62 billion in wage concessions from the company's three labor unions.[21] But because American delayed a filing with the Securities & Exchange Commission regarding executive-retention packages worth millions of dollars for forty-five executives until the union negotiations were completed, the company breached the uneasy trust between management and labor that Carty had spent years trying to repair. American issued a statement saying labor leaders had been informed of the retention package but did not tell their members. Labor leaders went ballistic, since it turned out this statement was not true. When American later retracted its statement, the gap of credibility widened even further. Carty then issued an apology saying, "It was not my intent to mislead anyone." He acknowledged, "my mistake was failing to explicitly describe these retention benefits, and because of that, many employees felt they were kept in the dark."[22] The apology rang hollow. Carty's credibility was gone. And within six days of these developments, so was he.

Understand that this attribute is different from being decisive: it's all about being honest and ethical. Organizations built on anything but the truth will eventually develop divisions within the leadership structure, and this division will become their fatal weakness.

When New York Yankees owner George Steinbrenner made a statement about a player's future that contradicted what four-time World Series champion manager Joe Torre had told the player, Torre was furious. It's one thing to have an owner micro-managing the day-to-day running of a team. But what upset Torre even more than the interference was the appearance that Torre was not telling the truth to his player. Torre's credibility was threatened. He responded immediately and publicly by explaining the series of events and setting the record straight, rightly believing it more important to maintain his credibility than risking dismissal.[23]

If you'd like one more reason to tell the truth, consider the instant availability of information. The Internet has made it easier than ever to expose lies, misrepresentations, and half-truths, and the news media's insatiable hunger for controversy will expose fraud, deceit, and self-dealing in a very public and humiliating way. Don't think for a minute you can evade or cover up the truth, because you can't.

More than two hundred years ago, founding father Thomas Paine said, "Character is easier kept than recovered." So always tell the truth, no matter how painful it may seem at the time.

Articulate

You must articulate solid principles coupled with your perspective on where the organization finds itself and where it needs to go. It's your responsibility to articulate the values, vision, and vigor that will be required to guide the organization through the uncertainty that accompanies change as you and your team move toward success.

Communication and inspiration are a little like the chicken and the egg. Which comes first?

I've placed "articulate" before "aspirational" because many great leaders have built successful companies by communicating clearly and honestly, without a lot of hype, fanfare, or even charisma. Such leaders communicate in a straightforward and factual manner. They do a terrific job of explaining the company's values, its mission, and what's expected of everyone.

Communicating may not come naturally to you. But you must do it, especially in times of change. As you communicate, what you say and how you say it must reflect your values and your style, otherwise your efforts will be perceived as false or "big hat, no cattle." When you give that impression, you've taken a step backward.

Communicating is hard work. "It takes three weeks to write a good impromptu speech," Mark Twain said. Kidding aside, you must make communicating a priority and devote your time to making it happen. Changing times cry out for clear, consistent, and constant communication. Study after study shows that it's virtually impossible to overcommunicate anytime, but particularly in times of change.

Kip Tindell, chief executive of The Container Store, a company ranked in the top ten of *Fortune*'s one-hundred-best-companies list, believes in overcommunication despite the risks.

> Overcommunicating ensures that our values and standards are consistent at every store. I know that sometimes [information] falls into the wrong hands, but we know that most retailers can't react to it, plus it's more important to communicate everything to our employees than to sit around worrying about what the competition gets. We've made the right choice by overcommunicating to all employees. [24]

In his sixty-five years in Parliament presiding over two world wars and the cold war, Winston Churchill stood at the forefront of change. He used his platform to tell his peers and the people of Great Britain where things stood and what more needed to be done to come out on the positive side of the crises they faced. It's been said that next to the Bible and Shakespeare, Churchill is the most frequent source of quotations. The number of words he wrote and spoke exceed those of virtually any writer in history. "Short words are best," he said, "and the old words when short are the best of all."

Churchill combined a rock-solid set of values, a bold vision, a terrific sense of humor, and a mastery of the English language to articulate his position. Consider Churchill's address to the Canadian House of Commons in December 1941. In language that is blunt and poetic, he frames England's position against the Axis powers of World War II and issues an all-encompassing challenge to those he seeks to rally behind his cause:

> We have not journeyed all the way across the centuries, across the oceans, across the mountains, across the prairies because we are made of sugar candy.
>
> We shall never descend to the German and Japanese level, but if anybody likes to play rough we can play rough, too. Hitler and his Nazi gang have sown the wind; let them reap the whirlwind.
>
> There is no room now for the dilettante, the weakling, for the shirker or the sluggard. The mine, the factory, the dockyard, the salt sea waves, the fields to till, the home, the hospital, the chair of the scientist, the pulpit of the preacher— from the highest to the humblest tasks, are all at equal honor, all have their part to play.[25]

Articulate your beliefs so that those who are important to you know exactly where you stand, where the company is headed, and what's expected of them.

Aspirational

Your principles should aspire to a cause, a goal, a vision.

When you're in charge in times of change, you must help the organization aspire toward a worthwhile goal that may at first seem unreachable. Like the best coaches, you must help your team aspire to greatness and then help them perform their best in order to attain the objective.

If you've visited Rome, the grandeur, craftsmanship, and permanence of the structures likely astonished you. The ancient Romans conceived of and then built this magnificent city in a swamp. From the Vatican and St. Peter's to the Colosseum and the Forum, the vision of the Roman emperors and clergy was grand and their execution superb. To think what they achieved utilizing the crudest technology is to stand in awe of their aspirations and accomplishments more than two millennia later.

The sheer scale of the Romans' planning and execution served, in most cases, three important purposes. And their larger-than-life approach to what historians say was essentially a blank sketch pad of a village provides you with important benchmarks and lessons to consider as you ponder the grandness of your own aspirations and those of the organization as you lead through change.

First, the Romans aspired on a grand scale. Their ability to think in big and bold terms ensured that the structures they erected and the streets they developed could accommodate an increasing number of people, vehicles, and animals as the city grew in size and stature. The Colosseum, for instance, built in 72 AD, covers nearly three football fields at the major axis of its layout. Its height towers to approximately 150 feet (comparable to a 15-story building), and can hold up to seventy thousand people. The lesson: *Ask if you're thinking big enough or if there's room to stretch your vision some more.*

Second, the Romans built their structures to last. As a result, many of these structures are not only still standing, but they became models for centuries to come. The Colosseum is still considered an architectural and engineering marvel and has served as the model for large stadia for two millennia. The lesson: *Ask if your solution is a temporary one or if you've incorporated a long-term view as well.*

Third, the ancient Romans appreciated the importance of symbols. The size of the structures towered over the citizenry and visitors, standing as big, bold, near permanent reminders of the superiority of Rome and those who controlled it—the emperors and clergy. "I found Rome a city of bricks," Augustus Caesar said, "and left it a city of marble." The lesson: *Ask if you've considered the significant power a symbol can bring to your initiative.*

I don't know whether Donald Trump has any Roman blood in him, but he certainly understands the importance of scale. Whatever you may think of Trump the person, there's no denying that he has aspired to change the face of New York City with his various real estate projects—no small goal. "You've got to think, so you might as well think big," he says.

Thinking big is not enough, however. Aspiration involves commitment to change for the better. Our firm will not take on an engagement unless we know leaders are committed to meaningful change. The leaders we work with must demonstrate a willingness to change and a will to succeed.

In good times and in tough times, strategies, programs, and people change. Sometimes even the business itself must undergo a major overhaul. The trick is to change practices without changing principles. This, of course, assumes your principles are where they ought to be.

The leadership of five enormous companies that lost sight of honorable principles reads like the FBI's "most wanted" list: Bernie Ebbers at Worldcom, Dennis Kozlowski at Tyco, Richard Schrushey at HealthSouth, Joe Berardino at Arthur Andersen and what appears to be most of the senior hierarchy at Enron. A company whose aspiration is to grow by acquisition is not automatically doomed to fail. But when honesty is sacrificed for personal gain, watch out.

CNN is recognized the world over as a superior source of round-the-clock news. Yet in 1978, the idea of starting Cable

News Network was a cross between laughable and risky. The proposal for an all news format presented to Ted Turner was similar to a proposal that had already been rejected by Time Inc.'s HBO subsidiary. But Turner thought grandly, had done his homework and saw an opportunity. His was a $100 million gamble that could have forced his company into bankruptcy. Yet he aspired to shoot for the stars. Turner's vision, speed and guts turned CNN from an idea into "the most trusted name in news."

One of the difficulties of leading through change is knowing who's really on board and who's faking it. You must find and keep people who share your beliefs, work ethic, and dreams. Trying to impose your values and enthusiasm on otherwise competent people is a short-term fix and a long-term problem. It won't work. Those people that do not share your aspirations need to leave.

Innovation is a component of being aspirational. Incremental innovation is a practice that builds on past successes. You see it a lot in grocery store aisles with new packaging and so-called line extensions, such as adding a new flavor or ingredient to an original recipe, or modifying a package to make it more customer-friendly. Those little improvements can result in big boosts to the bottom line. Even so, great leaders will aspire to the innovation breakthrough. We will examine innovation in depth in chapters 20 and 21, so one example will suffice here.

In 2000, Microsoft leaders met to discuss where the next big growth market would be and how they would help drive it and profit from it. To say they were aspirational in their thinking is an understatement. They decided to target the forty-five million small- and mid-size businesses worldwide, an initiative they figured would require investing billions of dollars and hiring hundreds of new employees. Within ten years of hatching this bold plan, Microsoft executives believe they will generate $10 billion in revenue from this freshly tapped market, up from just $300 million in 2003.[26]

Being aspirational incorporates a willingness to take calculated risks and to capitalize on opportunities. To be sure, in changing times, there are plenty of diamonds-in-the-rough and plenty of opportunities that are nothing more than lumps of coal. Choose wisely. We'll examine the whys and hows of goal setting and "possibility thinking" in chapters 10 and 11.

As you strive to be the best at what it is you do, be sure your goals are honorable and carry the potential to be embraced by all who want to succeed.

Set the bar high, starting with yourself.

Practical

No matter how lofty your goals, you must leaven them with a dose of practicality. Nothing saps the morale of an organization more than the belief that its stated goal is unattainable. So it's up to you to get your team focused on the practical implementation of its mission in order to deliver a positive outcome.

"A leader's job," said Gen. Peter Pace, vice chairman of the Joint Chiefs of Staff, "is understanding where you are, where you need to be, and using your energy to get to where you're going."[27] He believes it's not your job to worry about how you got into your current position. The real issue is *What are you going to do to improve your position?*

In a lengthy interview with *The New York Times* published shortly after he handed the chief executive responsibilities to Sam Palmisano, Lou Gerstner talked about the importance of being practical and executing a plan. At the time Gerstner took over at IBM in 1993, he said, "The last thing IBM needs now is a vision."[28] Gerstner sized up the organization quickly and concluded there was a "tendency to debate and argue every issue to the highest level of abstraction" so that "the process almost became one of the elegance of the definition of the problem rather than the actual execution of an action."[29] Gerstner feared a discussion of vision would turn into "a year-long debate."[30] The company, he believed, urgently needed an action plan. The interview provides an insightful glimpse of the "unsentimental pragmatism"[31] Gerstner brought to IBM. It's a quality that not only saved the company from possible bankruptcy but also returned it to preeminence.

Practical leaders base their decisions on facts, not emotion. But it's harder for some than others to separate emotion from logic when making the tough decisions that so often accompany change. Emotion can be a powerful ally, and there are occasions when you can use emotion to your advantage in times of change. Just make sure you fully understand when you're making a decision based on emotion, and when you're making a decision based on facts. After all, "facts are stubborn things," said our country's second president, John Adams, "and whatever may be our wishes, our inclination, or the dictates of our passions, they cannot alter the state of facts and evidence."[32]

In changing times, performance matters more than ever. A changing marketplace creates discomfort and difficulties for some, openings and opportunities for others. As the Greek philosopher Epictetus said, "It is difficulties that show what men are."

Executives at Microsoft face difficulties head-on. They still run the company like a start-up, writes David Thielen in *The 12 Simple Secrets of Microsoft*. At Microsoft, keeping everyone thinking in start-up terms means all employees are focused on the bottom line, the end result. The company targets 100 percent penetration of every market it's in. There is no other mission statement. Every employee must know and believe they are pursuing every competitor. They are asked, *What are you going to do to increase market share?* In this type of culture, performance and practicality matter more than office size, working hours, or apparel. It's all about smarts and speed and results. Senior executives:

- Fire unnecessary people
- Reassign managers incapable of doing the work of the people they manage
- Meet problems with solutions, not excuses
- Call only those meetings that require decisions
- Otherwise use e-mail to move information around the company
- Measure everything by success, not by activity

Such approaches are practical and strip away excuses to help keep everyone focused. It's not about instilling fear. It's about doing what you agreed to do. "I tell my teammates that doing 100 percent is the minimum acceptable standard," says Dumas Simeus, chief executive of Simeus Foods International. "You should not expect to get a raise or be promoted for simply doing what is asked. Doing what is asked is 100 percent of your job. Doing more than you're asked, doing more than is required, is how you get ahead."[33]

Practical executives implement systems to measure and reward stellar performance, as well as to study and replicate the successes. You must know:

- Which systems are working and which ones aren't
- Which employees are performing and which ones aren't
- Which suppliers are meeting your standards and which ones aren't
- Which customers are profitable and which ones aren't

"God," as world-renowned architect Mies van der Rohe once remarked, "is in the details."

When asked the secret of his success, the eminently practical oil executive and millionaire J. Paul Getty begrudgingly replied, "Get up early. Work hard. Find oil."

Whatever you conceive, make sure you believe. Then you must achieve.

So be practical.

Decisive

Being decisive means making the best decision you can make at the time and moving on.

In changing times, it may seem as if there's no end to the decisions that must be made. Your job, of course, is to make the ones that really count. Tom Engibous, chairman of Texas Instruments, says, "Good times are made by hard work and tough decisions in bad times."

There are elements of clarity, courage, and commitment in sound decisions:

- Clarity to understand the problem and the options for resolving it
- Courage to have the guts to actually verbalize what must be done
- Commitment to carry out the decision

Davy Crockett's two-hundred-year-old adage—"Be sure you're right, then go ahead"—remains apt advice today for executives and companies that can't seem to pull the trigger on their ideas. Whether some leaders lack clarity, courage, or some combination of the two is an open question. But it's not unusual in times of change to watch paralysis set in among senior leaders as they ponder a tough issue. In these situations, it's important to remember that doing nothing is a decision to take no action. Sometimes that can be fatal.

Medieval French philosopher Jacques Buridan, to illustrate the stumbling blocks associated with free will, posits: a starving dog is placed equidistant from two pieces of meat. The dog has no basis for choosing one piece of meat over the other and ends up starving to death.

Unfortunately, we've seen a few starving dogs in our day. A great number of businesses stagnate and lose their competitive footing as they waste time and spend money to get ready . . . to get ready . . . to get ready . . . to get ready. A classic example of companies getting ready but getting nowhere fast includes the Big Three automakers, who failed to recognize the gathering threat represented by the Japanese auto industry. They took years before deciding to design smaller, more fuel-efficient cars. The delay cost them billions of dollars. Today, of course, Japanese automobiles set the standard and even have manufacturing plants in the US.

Experimentation is appropriate, but in times of change you must quickly make a decision and implement it. So once the studying, testing, and soul-searching have been completed to the point where you have as much control as possible over the outcome of your decision, fire away and don't waste any time doing it.

The ability to make and act swiftly on key decisions is a defining quality of the best leaders. Erwin Rommel, the famed "Desert Fox" and the German commander most feared and respected by the Allies in World War II, wrote that the culminating characteristic of a battlefield commander is the "ability to think clearly and resolutely and, above all, fast. This sets the pace and determines the course of battle."[34]

Attila is another warrior who's probably regarded by many as nothing more than a barbarian or to others as an antihero. Yet under his leadership a group of nomadic peoples with little common purpose came together and confronted the mighty Roman Empire. Attila was a courageous and decisive leader—in war and in peace. He believed that every decision carried some risk but did not shirk from his duties as a leader. "Young chieftains must learn to be decisive," Attila wrote more than twenty-two hundred years ago.[35] It was vital to leaders, he continued, "knowing when to act and when not to act, taking into accounts all facts bearing on the situation and then responsibly carrying out their leadership role. Vacillation and procrastination confuse and discourage subordinates, peers and superiors and serve the enemy well."[36]

Confidant decision making accompanied by decisive action is a one-two punch that's important not just to generals on battlefields, but to any leader whose team faces change and looks for direction, assurance and wisdom.

President Harry Truman reflected on his ability to decide:

> All my life whenever it comes time to make a decision, I make it and forget about it, and go to work on something else, and when these things came before me as president of the United States, I made the decision on them, and went on to the next thing. You never have time to stop. You've got to keep going because there's always a decision just ahead of you that you've got to make, and you don't want to look back. If you make a mistake in one of these decisions, correct it by another decision, and go ahead.[37]

Ted Sorenson, special counsel in the Kennedy White House, codified what he considered the "ideal" decision-making process:

- First: agreement on facts
- Second: agreement on the overall policy objective
- Third: a precise definition of the problem
- Fourth: a canvassing of all possible solutions, with all their shades and variations
- Fifth: a list of all the possible consequences that would flow from each solution
- Sixth: a recommendation and final choice of one alternative
- Seventh: the communication of that selection
- Eighth: provision for its execution[38]

For those at all levels of an organization that are called upon to lead, for those who recognize how urgent it is for their companies to keep changing and improving, making big decisions comes with the territory. While the stakes sometimes are so high that your life might seem to pass before you, knowing that others have confronted equally difficult decisions can boost your confidence when it's your turn to decide.

Make your decision and move on.

Disciplined

Whereas being decisive is determining the action that must be taken, being disciplined means having the mental, moral, and physical temperament to execute your decision.

"Discipline," said George Washington, "is the soul of an army. It makes small numbers formidable, procures success to the weak, and esteem to all."[39] From discipline emerge direction, order, focus, and the freedom to be your best.

Great leaders use discipline as an anvil on which to hammer out their organization's identity and, ultimately, its value to others.

Consider this proposition: "Good, fast, cheap. Pick any two." Ever heard this line? What images come to mind? On which combinations do you and your business focus?

The proposition asserts that you cannot be all things to all people. Woe to those who try. The universal application of the "good, fast, cheap" idea is that an organization can succeed when it understands what its customers value most and then focuses its best efforts on delivering that value. A successful organization:

- Disciplines itself to stay true to delivering customer value
- Hires and promotes people who can consistently deliver it
- Tailors and produces its products or services to meet customer expectations
- Prices its products or services accordingly

Moreover, a disciplined organization does not pursue prospective customers who do not place the same value on its products or services as its best customers.

A successful organization can wed its reputation so firmly to a standard of excellence that its name becomes synonymous with the best attributes its particular industry has to offer. By its discipline, it becomes the "gold standard" for every other organization in its category. Take the high-end market, for instance. Retailing? Neiman-Marcus. Automobiles? Mercedes-Benz. Watches? Rolex. Education? Harvard. Chocolates? Godiva.

The "good, fast, cheap" saying proclaims a promise. Companies that deliver good products fast take the attitude that, *"We will meet our customers' high expectations quickly, conveniently, and cheerfully, and we will proudly ask for and receive a premium price for this experience."*

On the other hand, there's certainly nothing wrong with making price leadership the cornerstone of your organization. A cost-leadership strategy that emphasizes low prices requires just as much discipline as other strategies. Hundreds of successful enterprises maintain such discipline in their operations that they can compete and win by offering their customers great experiences and low prices. Retailing? Wal-Mart. PCs? Dell. Shipping? UPS. Fast food? McDonald's. Air travel? Southwest Airlines, whose motto is: "Twenty-five years. One mission. Low fares."

Discipline requires the courage to forfeit other opportunities. Consider John Alexander, former vice president at Emery Air Freight, who oversaw for fourteen years the customer-service function of the company's domestic and international accounts. At the beginning of his career his large office sought a broad-based sales strategy. Because of the high number of individual accounts, customer-service telephone calls were double the individual shipment count each day. When promoted to a smaller office, Alexander noticed similar activity. The Salt Lake City office processed an average of twelve outgoing domestic shipments per day and three international shipments per week. Inbound shipments averaged thirty-five per day. Upon gaining four large clients, he discovered a tremendous efficiency inherent with any one account. A large account with thirty bills of lading generally required only two customer-service contacts each day. This in turn positively affected other administrative and operational activities.

Alexander decided to focus that office's resources on only the biggest accounts. When confronted with skepticism about putting all of the company's eggs in a few baskets, Alexander readily admitted he was doing exactly that—and watching those baskets like a hawk. His approach paid off handsomely for Emery as the company tripled its volume and recorded increases in customer satisfaction and profits on its largest customers. In less than six months, his office consistently processed 125 domestic, twenty-five international, and seventy-five inbound shipments per day. "You can busy yourself with lots of customers that chew up your time," Alexander told me, "or achieve grand efficiencies with a few big ones." Such focus, he warned, does not come from being overly concerned about the profitability of individual transactions, but rather about adopting and then adhering to a disciplined approach that pays off at a higher level. His disciplined approach fast-tracked Alexander up Emery's corporate ladder toward the presidency, before he decided he'd rather run his own business. In 1989, Alexander founded Inventory Dynamics, where his relentless focus on service and profitability has resulted in a successful business representing blue-chip clients who appreciate and pay top dollar for the company's services.

As leaders push their organizations forward with discipline, they probe, explore, test, and sometimes even second-guess their lieutenants, especially in times of change. *What are your priorities? Where is the focus? What return on our investment should we expect from this initiative? How do the test results compare with our expectations?* Is the leader questioning? Always. Open to new ideas? You bet. Curious? Certainly. But always resolutely focused on the objective.

A disciplined leader must be discerning and selective about:

- The company's focus
- His or her own time
- Where to turn for counsel
- What ideas are adopted

A disciplined leader knows that too many "good ideas" can kill a company. You must avoid the trap of changing for change's sake.

Guard yourself so that you do not become enamored in the latest fad or strategy du jour. You must constantly question whether what you and others are doing will help you accomplish your objectives. Perhaps more so in changing times than in good times, you must stay focused on doing what is most important for the overall good of your organization—not just for today, but also for tomorrow.

A life without discipline is like a cup with no bottom—it can never be filled.

Focus, focus, focus.

Responsible

One of the differences between great leaders and marginal managers is the way in which they handle the responsibility that comes with their position. It's certainly important how you handle yourself in good times. But it's particularly important—and revealing—how you conduct yourself in times of change and adversity.

Right or wrong, leaders at the top of an organization get the credit when things go smoothly, and they get the blame when things go south. Sooner or later you're going to do something that does not go according to your plans and may even reflect poorly on you or the organization. When that happens, take the heat. "Always acknowledge a fault frankly," said Mark Twain. "This will throw those in authority off their guard and give you opportunity to commit more."

Twain's comment shouldn't be played purely for laughs. There are two serious thoughts wrapped inside his jab at authority. First, even leaders who are chief executives or the owners of their businesses must answer to a higher authority. For the chief executive, it's the board. For the owner, it could be his or her investors.

Moreover, beyond such external human authorities stands one's own conscience, and still beyond that, a higher spiritual authority. Many successful leaders are led as much by their faith in a higher being and, therefore, a higher purpose, as they are by sound business principles. Examples include:

- Warren Buffett and Berkshire Hathaway
- Tom Landry and the Dallas Cowboys
- The Haggars and Haggar Clothing Company
- Roger Staubach and The Staubach Company
- Mary Kay Ash and Mary Kay Cosmetics

Mary Kay Ash believed in and acknowledged a higher spiritual authority. Mary Kay Cosmetics was formed in 1963 with her life savings of $5,000, the help of her twenty-year-old son, Richard Rogers, and a deep responsibility to treat people fairly. The Golden Rule was her guiding philosophy, and she encouraged employees and members of her independent sales force "to prioritize their lives with God first, family second and career third." The company she founded on her strong faith and those timeless principles remains one of the greatest success stories in the history of business. Mary Kay Cosmetics has been named to *Fortune*'s 100 Best Companies list, and today eight hundred thousand consultants represent the company in thirty-seven countries.[40] Wholesale sales in June 2003 reached $134 million, the highest in the company's forty-year history, and its revenue for 2003 exceeded 2002's record of $1.6 billion wholesale.[41]

The second important thought implicit in Twain's jest is the importance of admitting—quickly, truthfully, and objectively—a shortcoming and accepting the consequences in order to get back in the race. It's harder to find fault with someone who admits he's made a mistake than it is with someone who tries to cover it up or blame it on others. Good leaders know when they've messed up; they admit it, regret that it occurred, are committed to learning from the mistake, and plan not to repeat it. Conversely, a leader who is unable to see or unwilling to acknowledge a mistake will not be effective. As we've already noted, a leader's credibility is key. Just as leaders who consistently underperform must be replaced, a leader with a pattern of failing to accept responsibility is a cancer that must be removed.

In what has been called her Golden Speech of 1601—one of the last addresses she made to Parliament—Queen Elizabeth said that, "To be a king and wear a crown is a thing more glorious to them that see it than it is pleasant to them that bear it."[42] Right and wrong, she believed, are eternal and absolute principles. Unfortunately, human beings are not absolute and, therefore, not automatically virtuous. They choose how to act, so they must accept the consequences. Elizabethan scholars point out that Elizabeth grounded her view of leadership in a full acceptance of responsibility.

More than 350 years after Elizabeth's reign, Max De Pree made similar observations about responsible leadership. De Pree is chairman emeritus of Herman Miller, Inc., a member of *Fortune* magazine's National Business Hall of Fame, a member of the advisory board of the Peter F. Drucker Foundation for Nonprofit Management, and the author of four books on leadership. "The first responsibility of a leader," he said, "is to define reality. The last is to say 'thank you.' In between the two, the leader must become a servant and a debtor. A friend of mine characterized leaders simply like this: 'Leaders don't inflict pain, they bear pain.'"[43]

The Bay of Pigs fiasco—the failed attempt in the early 1960s to invade Cuba to seek to overthrow Fidel Castro—was a huge black eye for the Kennedy administration. Years later, Ted Sorenson, President Kennedy's special counsel, noted that some favorable developments came out of that failure. Positive changes were made, Sorenson recalled, in the areas of policy, procedure and personnel. Sorenson observed that,

> the American people were absolutely astounded by [Kennedy's] willingness to take responsibility for the Bay of Pigs. Here was a plan that he had inherited. He could have blamed it on his predecessor, he could have blamed it on the holdover officers in the CIA and in the Pentagon, but instead he stood

up at a press conference and said, "This is my responsibility: I'm the officer in charge, and we're going to investigate and find out what went wrong, and make sure it doesn't happen again." And as a result, his standing in the popularity polls went up, which caused him some wry amusement.[44]

Great leaders accept responsibility for all the actions of those they lead.

Respectful

Read most any annual report these days and somewhere in the chief executive's letter to shareholders will be the thought that *our people are our most important asset.* Private companies tend to say the same thing, though in mission statements rather than annual reports.

If people are so important, why does morale tend to suffer during periods of change? Studies have shown that morale does in fact suffer at most organizations in times of change. It does so for three key reasons. First, leaders fail to paint a clear picture of the situation, the objective, and the steps that must be taken to achieve the objective. Second, leaders fail to articulate precisely the role of each person in the organization. Third, leaders fail to hold each person accountable for the performance that is expected and agreed upon.

So what do morale and respect have to do with one another? Everything.

In each of the three steps where a breakdown in leadership occurred, the element of respect was missing. Failure to paint an honest picture disrespects employees' intelligence. Sooner or later, people will figure out whether an executive is shooting straight or feeding them a line. "All [employees] really want you to do is tell the truth, tell it like it is so they can digest it, deal with it and be prepared for whatever happens," says Patricia Lucent, the chief executive directing Lucent's turnaround.[45]

Failure to tell employees what's expected of them in clear, simple terms disrespects their abilities. Tell them how they must perform and how they will be measured. Either they're good enough to do the job (why would you have hired them if they weren't?), or they're not (why would you keep them otherwise?). Give them the direction, the resources, and the responsibility, and allow them to perform. Either you trust them or you don't.

Failure to hold a person accountable disrespects the rest of the organization because it sends a signal that poor performance counts the same as great performance. It disrespects the person who underperforms, because it lulls that person into believing his subpar performance is superb. It also disrespects the leader because it's a blow to credibility.

James MacGregor Burns, a Pulitzer Prize-winning biographer of President Franklin Roosevelt, writes, "In real life, the most practical advice for leaders is not to treat pawns like pawns, nor princes like princes, but all persons like persons." Humorist Dave Barry says that, "A person, who is nice to you, but rude to the waiter, is not a nice person. This is very important. Pay attention. It never fails."

Yet, too often, executives play favorites. Worse yet, many executives believe that they can get the most out their employees through fear, public humiliation, or intimidation. "The floggings will continue until morale improves," goes the old line, but it's hard to build and sustain a business on fear. At some point in his or her career, everyone will face a peer, a boss, or an investor like this. But the chances are low those people are respected. The chances are even lower that most employees will stick around for very long to work for or with someone like this.

A better approach emphasizes respect: "Treat a person as he is and he will remain as he is. Treat a person as if he were what he could be and should be, and he will become what he could and should be."

Numerous psychological studies support the effectiveness of positive reinforcement. It's called the Pygmalion Effect, named after the mythological sculptor Pygmalion, who fashioned the ideal woman from ivory and then fell in love with her. Venus brought the statue to life, and the couple lived happily ever after. Positive reinforcement is also called the psychology of self-fulfilling prophecy. In the movie *My Fair Lady*, Professor Henry Higgins transforms a Cockney flower girl into a duchess simply by changing her surroundings, her attire, her speech, and her perspective on life.

That's great in fairy tales and movies, you might say. But does that approach really work for leaders looking for more productivity in times of change? Yes.

Years ago, a Dr. King at Tulane University conducted a study with unskilled laborers taking a welding class. Dr. King told the welding instructor that certain individuals had the talent to become outstanding welders, whereas others had no aptitude for welding because they lacked the eye-hand coordination and intelligence. The welding instructor accepted Dr. King's statements as fact when, actually, Dr. King was lying. Dr. King had picked all of the individuals at random and had no information about their ability to become welders. But because the instructor treated the students in the class according to his expectations, that's how they turned out. The ones he believed had high potential received his individual attention and encouragement. They scored the highest on their final exams. The ones the instructor didn't expect to excel received only a fraction of his individual time, were not encouraged, and scored very low on their exams.[46]

One reason sports coaches are often viewed as models for business leaders to emulate is because the best coaches do, in fact, get the most out of their players. With nothing to hide behind except the performance of the team and a won-lost record, a good coach must not only earn the respect of his or her team but return that respect to the players.

Jimmy Johnson coached the Miami Hurricanes to a national championship and the Dallas Cowboys to two Super Bowl victories. He's the only coach to achieve championships at both the college and professional levels of football. Johnson, therefore, is regarded as a master motivator and a coach who respects his players' talents. He knows all about the Pygmalion Effect and uses tough love to bring out players' potential. Johnson explains the importance of being sincere and consistent:

> Whether I'm treating the individual player as a true winner, or treating the team as if they're going to win, or treating the assistant coach as if he is in my opinion the brightest, hardest working coach in the league, I do it with the scientific knowledge that if you treat people that way, long enough and sincerely enough, then more times than not, that's what you'll get from the person. Even if you don't attain the final goal, at least the treatment will have such a positive influence that he'll come closer to attaining the goal than he would have otherwise.
>
> Sincerity is the most important component of positive treatment. The critical factor in proving sincerity is consistency. You can't say, "This person I'm going to treat positively, and this person negatively, and this person I'm not going to pay any attention to." You can't turn it off and on. I think you've got to treat everyone that way.
>
> Everybody says you have to coach according to your own personality. But I think you've got to take it one step further: You've got to be able to control your personality. In order to get the optimal response, you have to be strong enough mentally that you can govern how positive, and how sincere, and how negative you are. You can't be controlled by outside situations.[47]

During the economic downturn that began in the spring of 2000, many chief executives were tested. Declining market share shrank revenue, which shrank budgets, which shrank headcount, which shrank stock prices. This recession hit almost every business leader hard and many top leaders' jobs were on the line. Some executives dealt with the pressure better than others.

Respect, or the lack thereof, can lengthen or shorten an executive's tenure. Dick Brown of EDS and John Chambers of Cisco led their Fortune 100 technology companies at a time when their respective stock prices both plunged by more than 60 percent. The Cisco meltdown occurred in January 2001, while the EDS crisis hit in September 2002. The short-term results were disastrously similar, but the outcomes couldn't have been more different. At the time of their respective crisis, Chambers' Cisco and Brown's EDS lost billions of dollars of market capitalization value and millions of dollars in dividends to shareholders. Thousands of employees lost their jobs.

Why is Dick Brown no longer at EDS, while John Chambers remains at Cisco? Insiders and outsiders have repeatedly given the same answer. Because John Chambers treats people with respect, he is loved and admired. As a result, he received a second chance. "The board never wavered in its support for Chambers," says Robert Slater, who studied the company for months during its heyday and after its fall.[48] Because Dick Brown's tenure at EDS was marked by his harsh treatment of people and a failure to show respect consistently, he was feared and ultimately forced to resign. "Delivering bad news [to Dick Brown] was not a good thing," said one former EDS executive, "so you postponed it as long as you could."[49]

There's an old Navy saying that says, "Praise in public, punish in private."

Be tough, be fair, and always show respect for the individual.

Persistent

The bookends of great leadership are honesty and persistence.

By whatever name you choose to call it—persistence or passion, stubbornness or stamina, drive or determination—all great leaders demonstrate the will to win. They refuse to give up. A leader confronted with change, uncertainty, or adversity keeps finding a way to put one foot in front of the other. It's true today and it's been this way for thousands of years.

Nearly twenty-five hundred years ago, the Greek soldier Pheidippides was picked by his commander to deliver the news of a great victory over a Persian army of superior strength. "Rejoice. We conquer," Pheidippides gasped after running the twenty-two miles from the Bay of Marathon to Athens with the news. Having persevered through this hardship, his duty done, he promptly dropped dead. We remember and honor his feats of endurance and his ability to complete his task to this day. Fortunately, few of us run a marathon unless we're prepared, and fewer still will ever see our determination rewarded the same way as Pheidippides.

Nevertheless, persistence is a critical quality for leaders battling change. An entry from Ulysses S. Grant, commander of the Union Army in the Civil War and later president of the United States, stands as testimony to his exceptional stamina. It also underscores the fact that great leaders must draw from their personal reservoir of energy in times of difficulty. Writing that he and his baggage were separated six days previously, he "consequently had no change of underclothing, no meal except such as I could pick up sometimes at other headquarters, and no tent to cover me." Upon reaching Admiral David Dixon Porter's flagship in the evening, "the first thing I did was to get a bath, borrow some fresh underclothing . . . and get a good meal." After a quick conference with officers, Grant "wrote letters to the general-in-chief informing him of our present position, dispatches to be telegraphed, orders to General Sullivan commanding above Vicksburg, and gave orders to all my corps commanders. About twelve o'clock at night I was through my work and started for Hankinson's ferry, arriving there before daylight."[50]

He was ready for another hard day of decision-making, commanding and winning.

Great inventors are also inspirational examples of persistence. They must rebound from failure time and again before finally discovering the key that will unlock the mystery they face. Ever wonder where we'd be if scientists and inventors had simply given up after their first, second, or even third failure? If they can overcome setbacks, so can you.

Thomas A. Edison, whose most famous invention was the incandescent light bulb, patented 1,092 other inventions. Someone once remarked on the huge number of failures Edison had encountered in his search for a new storage battery—some fifty thousand experiments before achieving the desired results. "Results?" said Edison. "Why, I have gotten a lot of results. I know 50,000 things that won't work." A famously hard worker who could be found in his lab for up to twenty hours a day, Edison believed that, "Genius is one percent inspiration and 99 percent perspiration."

Texan Gail Borden persisted through almost twenty years of failure before finding success with his condensed milk breakthrough. In the 1840s, Borden began experimenting on various projects. They all failed. By 1849, he developed a dehydrated meat biscuit. Convinced of its utility, he bet his entire fortune of $100,000, and lost it all. Undeterred, Borden continued to pursue sales of meat biscuits, but the business failed, driving him to bankruptcy in 1852. In 1853 he applied for a patent on a process for condensing milk in vacuum. After a three-year wait, he was rewarded with American and British patents. Borden then turned his attention full-time on condensing milk. He opened a factory in Connecticut in 1856, but failed; then he tried and failed again in 1857. He secured new backing and opened another factory in Connecticut in 1858. When the Civil War brought intensified demand for condensed milk, Borden was an "overnight success."

You've probably heard the saying that "tough times don't last, but tough people do." Fifty-eight years after Borden's death, the Great Depression hit America hard and tested that truism again.

Ebby Halliday worked after-hours and weekends during her high school years in Abilene, Kansas, selling hats in the basement of a department store "at a time people could barely afford to eat," she says. "I graduated in 1929—the year every bank in America closed. The Great Depression was in full swing with bread lines around the corner, but I kept moving." And move she did, to Dallas in 1938. "I thought I had died and gone to heaven," she says. "The mayor had called an end to the Depression. There was confidence and enthusiasm. I was still selling hats . . . Over a seven-year period I accumulated $1,000—quite a sum in those days. I asked a doctor to advise me on the stock market. I told him I wanted to become an entrepreneur. He initially refused, saying 'I don't advise women because when they lose money they cry.' I said, 'Try me.' And with that, I parlayed my $1,000 into $12,000 and opened my own shop." Later, the husband of one of Ebby's regular customers said, "if you can sell those crazy hats, maybe you can sell these 52 experimental homes on Walnut Hill Golf Course." The homes were built from reinforced concrete and were unlike any ever seen. "They were ugly," says Ebby, "so I decorated them and they became the first display homes. And I sold them." The rest, as they say, is real estate history. By 2004, Ebby Halliday Realtors had become the top-rated residential real estate company in Dallas and was ranked tenth nationally. "We've been up and down in our nearly 60 years in business, but we've been resilient, we've built our reserves, and we keep progressing—even when the market is dipping, so we're prepared for the end of a downturn. We have invested heavily in technology, and find that our competitors send their customers to our web site because we have the most complete and up-to-date listings."[51]

At some point, a fresh wave of doubt and problems will confront you as you near the completion of your goal. Don't be surprised. Don't be surprised if things that have never gone wrong before now go wrong. Don't be surprised if that is the occasion when critics begin to knock the project. Don't be surprised if your passion for the work suddenly evaporates. Just don't give up.

Of all the qualities Anne Mulcahy has brought to the incredibly difficult job of turning around Xerox, her will to win may be the biggest. In 2000, she inherited $17.1 billion in debt and $154 million in cash. The capital markets had dried up, seven consecutive quarters of losses loomed ahead, and an SEC investigation was under way. Layoffs had sapped morale, and the company's market cap had lost 90 percent of its value. While Mulcahy's reputation was above reproach, her pedigree did not remotely resemble those of other chief executives.[52] Nevertheless, she brought to her challenge of restoring profit and respect to Xerox attributes that have been AWOL from many corner offices these days. Mulcahy is described as "straightforward, hard-working, disciplined . . . fiercely loyal to Xerox . . . [and] stubborn."[53] While she and Xerox are not out of the woods, Anne Mulcahy has kept Xerox alive in the toughest three years of the company's forty-five-year history. "Sometimes you can will your way through things," Mulcahy says. "As much as you need competence, luck and hard work, I think will has a lot to do with it."[54]

Howard Davis, the chief executive of Tracy-Locke and, at the time, the youngest leader of a major national advertising agency, navigated his company through a series of acquisitions he initiated, bringing unprecedented expansion and unprecedented success for clients such as Pepsi-Cola, Taco Bell, Frito-Lay, and Phillips Petroleum Company. It was not always easy. He once gave each of his lieutenants (of which I was one) a framed quote from President Calvin Coolidge to remind them of the value of persistence: "Press on," the quote from Coolidge read. "Nothing in the world can take the place of persistence. Talent will not; nothing is more common than unsuccessful men with talent. Genius will not; unrewarded genius is almost a proverb. Education alone will not; the world is full of educated derelicts. Persistence and determination alone are omnipotent."

In times of change, take heart and learn from leaders of all descriptions from across the ages who have stared adversity of some sort in the face and refused to quit.

As Churchill said, "Never give in—never, never, never, never, in nothing great or small, large or petty, never give in except to convictions of honour and good sense."

"Try as we might, sir, our team of managment consultants has been unable to find a single fault in the manner in which you conduct your business. Everything you do is a hundred per cent right. Keep it up! That will be eleven thousand dollars."

8

Invest in Yourself to Be Your Best

Earlier, I touched on the benefits of creating a SWAT team of trusted advisors to help you as you lead your company in times of change.

Depending on the rigors of your job, the pressures you face, and your experience handling change, you may want to consider an executive coach—either as part of your most trusted circle of advisors or outside it.

As a senior executive, you've achieved success based largely on your attitude, abilities, and acuity. Your skills have been your transport to your position in life. The thought of needing a coach can seem bush league. But the fact is, coaching elite-level athletes is really no different than coaching elite-level executives. It's been said that Tom Landry's job as the head coach of the Dallas Cowboys was to get grown men to do things they didn't want to do in order to achieve something they all desperately wanted. That's the essence of coaching.

And that's why it's helpful to have a wise, objective, focused, and—occasionally—unmerciful evaluation of your personal strengths, weaknesses, opportunities, and threats (SWOTs). As we've already discussed, knowing where you are is the first step in keeping "excellence" excellent.

At a time when anyone can hang out a coaching shingle, how do you find a resource that won't waste your time or money? Like anything in life, you must define your needs, evaluate solutions, and execute. A good first step is taking a quick look at what executive coaching is and is not.

Coaching Is:	Coaching Is Not:
Tough love	Sycophantic
Motivation and mentoring	Therapy
A sounding board	Personality-based
Performance assessment	Theoretical
Empowerment	Political maneuvering
Removing roadblocks	Focused on externals
Unlocking potential	Making you into someone you're not
Identifying and filling gaps	Manipulation
Practice and rehearsal	Memorization

Specific individual development needs are unique. Consider these questions:

- Are you experiencing professional frustration?
- Are you stuck on a career plateau?
- Are you unclear about why you're not moving upward and forward?
- Are you bored? Disenchanted?
- Have you lost passion for your work?
- Are you less comfortable in social settings?

- Does public speaking cause anxiety?
- Do your management or leadership skills need sharpening?
- Are you facing challenges you've never faced?
- Is your change curve steeper than your ability to adjust?

Take a few minutes and identify specific barriers, limitations, challenges, and development goals you want to address. As you're cataloging your needs, remember the old saying that executives get hired for their skills but they get fired for their personalities.

The proliferation in the number of executive coaches, coaching accreditation organizations, and coaching web sites can confuse your search for a coach. To complicate things further, many coaches don't even refer to themselves as "coaches." You may find terms such as career strategists, executive development consultants, life strategists, performance consultants, personal improvement consultants . . . ad nauseum. Like most searches for providers of professional services, your best source is your own network of peers and their referrals. More of your peers are using coaches than you might think. So tap into your network and leave advertising and Internet searches to others.

Here are seven points to consider in finding and working with an executive coach:

1. A Good Coach Offers a Free Initial Consultation

Set a face-to-face meeting, and bring your list of needs to discuss. Don't try to shortcut this step with a phone call because you want to watch them and examine their body language as they listen to you.

2. Communication and Understanding Are Key

Is the coach tuned into your specific needs or simply trying to force-fit you into a methodology and process he or she has used a thousand times before? Test your candidates with specific scenarios to see how the two of you will work together.

3. Select a Coach who Works with People Like You

Look for a coach who's worked with other executives at a similar career stage. Perhaps gender is an influence.

4. Don't Get Hung up on Professional Credentials

Ability, experience, and rapport are more important. A coach with a psychology background and no business experience may be just what you need to remove interpersonal barriers; conversely, a person with strong business acumen and no formal psychology background may be the ideal person to help you develop those same goal-setting and discipline objectives.

5. Make Sure Your Coach Will Give You Blunt Feedback

The last thing you need is a "yes"-spouting coach.

6. Know Your End Game

Be specific about your goals and the time period in which you want to achieve your goals so that your work is focused, directed, and measurable.

7. You Should Drive Your Development Process

Your coach is just that . . . a coach.

● ● ●

Effective coaches will guide you through a process consisting of four fundamental components:

- An examination of the "real you"
- An examination of outside forces
- An analysis of where these points converge and diverge
- A plan for moving forward

The time, effort and money you spend with an executive coach should result in significant improvement in your performance and career/life satisfaction. Plus, you should start seeing results and insights in a relatively short time. Investing the time and effort up front to find yourself the right coach will give you greater insight into your development needs and will help keep your game at the elite level.

Think of it as an investment that pays dividends every day of your life.

"*Give it to me straight, Doc. How long do I have to ignore your advice?*"

9

Know When to
Call in a Doctor

There's another set of resources beyond the executive coach that you may want to consider investing in as you seek to fix a problem or capitalize on change: outside consultants. Sometimes you and your team need more firepower than you, your staff, or your regular advisors can provide.

But don't make a move to bring in an outside consultant until you're ready to "take the medicine."

You've heard the one about the patient that says, "Doctor, it hurts when I do this." The doctor says, "Then don't do that." You smile at this little joke and think, "How silly."

But it's not funny when executives hire consultants to help them fix problems yet refuse to make recommended changes after being told the equivalent of "don't do that." Why would smart business leaders hire consultants in the first place? And then why would they not follow the advice for which they are paying so dearly in terms of time, energy, and money?

The first—and biggest—step in fixing a problem or capitalizing on an opportunity is to determine if the issue is real. I've found that leaders must reach a certain threshold of pain or, conversely, must quantify the unfulfilled potential before true change is possible.

The second step is determining whether your team can address the situation satisfactorily. If you have a legal matter and you're not an attorney, you'll probably retain a lawyer to help you with your case. Ditto if you have a significant health concern, and you're not a doctor. But there's a great divide between doctors and lawyers (a species of consultants) and other consultants. Outside specialists must demonstrate to you that they are qualified to help you and your organization achieve a positive outcome.

It's natural for you to want to lead your existing staff in a process to address these issues rather than calling in consultants. But it's smart business to hire outsiders when the answer is "no" or "I'm not sure" to any part of this question: "Do I and my staff have the time, experience, skill, and third-party objectivity to address this issue capably?"

Leaders that engage outside consultants can expect to reap four benefits. First, outsiders are usually viewed as a neutral resource with little, if any, baggage. Their sole objective is producing a positive outcome for the organization. Second, expecting any decision maker involved in the planning process to think, listen, watch meeting dynamics, include reluctant participants in the discussion, take notes and keep a strategy meeting on topic and on time while keeping their personal biases in check is unrealistic. It can't be done effectively. Third, an outsider carries no preconceived notions of what can or cannot be done by an organization. A fresh perspective may help leaders reconsider ideas they've previously taken for granted or dismissed. Fourth, unlike staffers with other daily responsibilities, outsiders are dedicated to developing a high quality plan and reducing it to writing within the shortest possible time.

Typically, consultants are retained to help organizations:

- Bring a fresh perspective to an issue and identify new possible solutions
- Assess an issue objectively and the organization's ability to address it
- Augment existing staff to accelerate a positive outcome
- Apply experience to minimize mistakes, decrease costs, and increase effectiveness

- Provide discipline and accountability to implement new initiatives

Clients understand that consultants do not know their business better than they do. But there are fundamentals in any business— value propositions, systems, processes, programs, and people— that must be in place and working effectively for an enterprise to be successful. It's the consultant's job to identify any gaps, recommend solutions to close those gaps, and then ensure that agreed-upon initiatives are executed effectively.

After making the decision to hire a consultant, next determine the type of relationship you want. In *The Trusted Advisor*, David Maister identifies four levels of a client-consultant relationship:

1. Service-based (clients receive information)
2. Needs-based (clients receive solutions)
3. Relationship-based (clients receive ideas)
4. Trust-based (clients receive a "safe haven for hard issues")

When hiring consultants to provide information (i.e., "Help us quantify this emerging market") or a specific solution ("Help us launch a new product"), you're most interested in their experience, expertise, and examples of success. Relationship- and trust-based partnerships may begin as an information- or needs-based relationship but are built on reputation, time, and performance. The best relationships are two-way. That means the best consultants are also sizing you up before agreeing to help you address your problem or opportunity. Years ago, we at Bustin & Co. codified our firm's expectations:

- Is this a product or service we believe in?
- Do we believe in the organization's management and their motivation to make necessary changes?
- Is working for this organization of strategic value to our firm?
- Does this organization offer the opportunity to perform the type of work we want to do?

- Based on current staff, can we deliver the quality of work the firm and the client expect?
- Does this organization have adequate financial resources?
- Is the organization willing to pay the fees we believe are fair?

Lastly, you and your consultant should answer these five questions together before starting work:

1. What Outcome Do We Expect?

Be specific. You'll typically want to achieve

- Fresh perspective on an issue
- Agreement among senior management that "this is where we are, this is where we're going, and this is how we'll get there"
- A detailed implementation plan

2. What Process Will We Use?

Understand the steps of getting from point A to point B. Decide how much staff participation is appropriate. Most organizations want their people to be involved throughout the process. Good consultants encourage collaboration.

3. When Will We See the Deliverables?

Agree on milestones to confirm findings, discuss preliminary thinking, and review work product. Set a deadline and discuss exceptions to the time line.

4. How Much Will This Engagement Cost?

Beyond consulting fees, remember that staff time is a cost (i.e., time away from regular duties, overtime, lost opportunity). Failure to implement the plan after securing staff input is a cost to morale.

5. What Guarantee Do I Have That This Will Work?

None, if both parties have not been candid. None, if the consultant doesn't perform. None, if the organization is unwilling to change. Success occurs through collaboration, trust, and a mutual incentive to succeed.

● ● ●

Tolstoy said, "Everyone thinks of changing the world, but no one thinks of changing themselves."

Call a doctor when you're ready to take the medicine. Hire a consultant when you've decided you need a bit more firepower to help you and your team capitalize on change.

Part 3

Preparing Your Organization to Profit from Change

"*Sir, the following paradigm shifts occurred while you were out.*"

10

Building a Pyramid
Constructing a Framework for Change

Great leaders use the planning process as a framework to confront change, set a course of action, and secure buy-in throughout the organization.

More than five thousand years ago, ancient Egypt was emerging from a period of uncertainty and discontinuity and was becoming a unified nation-state. As the Egyptians adapted to the changes brought on by this unification, King Djoser commissioned the world's first pyramid about 2950 BC, establishing a reign of twenty-one years that is thought to have been politically and economically stable. The Greek historian Herodotus believed—and the Bible supports this belief—that the pyramids were constructed by slaves, but more recent evidence strongly suggests these wonders of the world were planned, designed, and built by a skilled workforce of thousands of volunteers led by the vizier, or head of state, who was tasked with building the king's pyramid.[55]

The pyramids—and the infrastructure surrounding their planning and construction—hold valuable lessons for leaders responsible for creating a framework within an organization that must address change, including insights to planning and implementing significant initiatives.

Your changes may not be as sweeping as those of an emerging civilization nor as grand as the design and construction of the pyramids, but times of change still make employees and bankers nervous and make investors impatient for innovation, growth, and profitability. In this chapter, we'll explore the pyramids to discover the principles that undergird effective planning. In the following chapter, we'll examine other lessons for taking specific steps to help you and your organization uncover or strengthen your competitive advantage.

The planning process is the single best way to prepare your organization to capitalize on change. When conducted effectively, the planning process:

- Breaks down barriers between departments, business units, and geographic regions so problems and opportunities are viewed holistically
- Brings focus to an issue
- Provides a safe harbor for what we call "possibility thinking"
- Achieves alignment among the senior management team
- Establishes specific objectives and a plan of action
- Helps motivate your team to implement the plan and achieve the objective

In well-run companies, the planning process is an annual or semi-annual mechanism for reviewing current situations, establishing objectives for the coming year and beyond, and plotting a course of action to accomplish the objectives. Such companies review performance against established objectives quarterly, monthly, and sometimes even weekly, at each phase making adjustments based on changing priorities and accomplishments to date.

To oversimplify, there are two basic approaches to planning. One process is a budget-based approach where the current budget is a platform upon which the next year's plans and financials are built. The second process is a zero-based method that approaches planning from more of a management-by-objective perspective.

The best companies, although interested in budgeting, leverage the planning process to give them something more.

They see the planning process as a springboard to identify and evaluate new opportunities, consider new strategies, and discuss objectives that may at first seem unattainable. It's a process emphasizing planning first and budgeting second. This type of planning requires more effort to view all aspects of your operation from a clean-slate perspective. This approach will also force you to confront uncomfortable realities, but when done right, it brings exhilaration, inspiration, and reward.

Principles of effective planning

As you and your team balance the need for fast, sustainable results against the strategic long-term interests of your business, keep the following four principles in mind as you undertake any strategic planning process:

1. Decide How Good You Want to Be

The ancient Egyptians considered it critically important that when they died "their physical body should continue to exist on earth, so they could progress properly through the afterlife," writes historian Dr. Aidan Dodson.[56] Because of this belief, "providing proper eternal accommodation for their body after they had died was very important to them."[57] Hence Egyptian leaders took every step possible to make their final resting place the best it could be. This is the first principle of effective planning: aim for excellence. Begin your planning process by aiming for excellence and examining opportunities for continuous improvement, rather than maintaining the status quo.

2. Resist Shortcuts

For a project as colossal as the design and construction of a pyramid, Egyptian leaders recognized that a methodical approach to achieving their objectives was not only necessary, but also smart. Consider the Great Pyramid, the base of which has been calculated to accommodate Britain's Houses of Parliament and St. Paul's Cathedral "with room to spare."[58] Such massive construction would take twenty- to twenty-five thousand workers laboring without such technology as steam, electrical power, or even pulleys "20 years or more."[59] To be sure, you don't have twenty years to address the changes confronting your organization. But emphasis on the tactical world of price cuts, flashy technologies, or new sales promotions can create a false sense of security that you are generating substantive results when you are not. "We're making things happen," some may say. True, but are they the right things? To make certain, think critically about your destination. Then think, as the ancient Egyptians did, about how long it will take to get there. Do not let a sense of urgency lead you into taking harmful shortcuts. Savvy leaders are focused and urgent, but they wisely counsel patience and resist quick, superficial fixes.

3. Recalibrate Your Objectives

Not all of the Egyptians' pyramids were successful structures. King Snefru built Egypt's first true, or straight-sided, pyramid about 2600 BC at Meidum, thirty miles south of Memphis. Historians say this project began as a stepped pyramid, and "as it neared its completion the steps were packed with stone and the whole structure was cased in finest limestone."[60] But the heavy outer casing collapsed. Undaunted, King Snefru commissioned a new design for a true pyramid at Dahshur. This project also was less than successful because its angle of ascent was too steep and had to be flattened, hence its name, "the Bent Pyramid."[61] Undaunted, Snefru commissioned a third pyramid. His Red Pyramid at Dahshur is considered a successful true pyramid, and, not coincidentally, it is also believed to be the king's final resting place.[62] The lesson for today's leaders is twofold. First, embrace change and make your planning process a time to measure performance from a new perspective. Reexamine priorities. Look for fresh insights. Scrutinize your go-to-market strategy. Determine new ways to solve your problems. Ensure that your team is aligned. Take a critical look at your people, processes, and programs. Listen to your customers and suppliers. Then adjust your plans to accommodate what you've learned. The second lesson is just as important. Never give up on moving forward to achieve your objective. You may need to set a new objective. But never give up.

4. Commit to Action

Ancient Egyptian kings who committed the best of their country's intellectual, physical, natural, and financial resources to building pyramids were rewarded with structures that solidified their leadership positions and contributed to their reputations. Effective planning, organization, and execution were critical to completing pyramid construction satisfactorily. Conversely, historians have seen that when the central control that characterized the Great Pyramid Age collapsed in Egypt's three intermediate periods (ca. 2125–1975, 1630–1520, 1075–715 BC), "few monuments were constructed and there was little political expansion."[63] In times of change, there can be an urge among those in charge to batten down the hatches in an effort to ride out the storm, but such thinking can backfire. Studies conducted through the American economic recessions of 1923, 1949, 1954, 1975, and 1991 overwhelmingly showed that companies that chose to maintain or increase aggressive marketing initiatives achieved better revenue growth and increased profit performance as compared with companies that made the decision to cut back.[64] Committing to fund R&D, marketing, and sales efforts in the face of an uncertain economy takes courage. Allen Questrom, chief executive of J. C. Penney, has it. While many retailers cut back in the face of the 2001 recession, Questrom announced he would commit an additional $100 million in advertising for the fourth quarter as part of his five-year turnaround plan.[65] As a result, Penney department stores are achieving success at a time when most other retailers are experiencing difficulty.[66] Once you commit your time to plan, be sure to commit your organization to act on your plans.

● ● ●

Southwest Airlines uses its annual planning process to identify new ways to make itself better. Each year, the company identifies between one and three corporate goals (e.g., "improve the airport experience"), and then this goal cascades down to departments that develop strategies, action items, and budgets, then on to all employees, then on to suppliers, and, ultimately, to customers. It's the type of planning, thinking, and implementation that has made Southwest Airlines number one in customer satisfaction for three consecutive years and a high flier on Wall Street.

"In preparing for battle," said Dwight D. Eisenhower, "I have always found that plans are useless, but planning is indispensable." With that one comment, the D-day general and US president summarized the paradox of planning. Plans are essential. If you don't know where you're going, any road will take you there. Still, circumstances can foil the best of plans. "We don't have time for planning. Why bother? We're busy executing and adapting." When you're up to you neck in alligators it's easy to forget the original objective was to drain the swamp.

In the previous chapter, we discussed the value of retaining outside consultants. Confronted with the paradox of planning, you may wish to turn to an outside resource to help drive the planning process.

The best planning exercises can be powerful tools for any organization, and they are critical for those wrestling with change and uncertainty. How one structures the planning process and moves forward to address the ideas, questions, and possibilities it raises often separates leaders from laggards.

"All men dream: but not equally," said T.E. Lawrence, better known as Lawrence of Arabia. "Those who dream by night in the dusty recesses of their minds wake in the day to find that it was vanity. But the dreamers of the day are dangerous men, for they may act their dream with open eyes, to make it possible."

By embracing uncertainty and using the planning process as a time of reexamination, renewal, and recommitment, you can begin to help your organization prepare to capitalize on change.

"How can we know who we are when the best marketing
consultants of our time don't know."

11

Uncovering Your Competitive Advantage

I n times of change, many executives play not to lose. Other leaders embrace changing times as an opportunity to build momentum and become stronger than ever.

When things are going well, there may be a temptation to maintain the status quo, to not rock the boat. Conversely, continued sales declines often necessitate cutting expenses and, perhaps, prices.

But the real question in both cases is, "What investments must we continue to fund to enhance our competitive advantage?" Cruising along on autopilot can be deadly. Cutting back on growth engines will not help you grow. Yet the urge to cut—rather than fund—growth engines during times of uncertainty is a powerful one.

Look at the hard-hit technology industry for two different approaches. Most technology companies responded to the soft market of 2000–2003 by cutting employees and investment spending. Only a few, like Apple, IBM, and Intel took the steps necessary to help define their own futures. One analyst noted that Apple's innovation helped generate strong earnings results amid the technology meltdown, saying the company's performance "shows that Apple dances to its own tune. If it has good products it doesn't matter what the PC market does."[67]

The difference in approaches, you may say, is size, cash flow, customer base, or product mix. Not true. "Economic results are earned only by leadership, not competence," says Peter Drucker in his 1964 book, *Managing for Results*. The difference between winners and also-rans is the commitment by executives to pursue, find, and implement new ways of unlocking the potential that exists within every business. In times of change and uncertainty, a well-thought-out planning process can be an effective way toward solidifying—or perhaps even uncovering—your competitive advantage.

What are the specific deliverables we want to achieve as an outcome of the planning process? How can we be sure that we won't just think up a lot of ideas that sound good but go nowhere? How will this planning process help us improve our marketplace position? How will this process help us to enhance our competitive advantage when we already know what makes us special?

How to Structure the Planning Process

Our firm's work with companies to address the opportunities of growth or the realities of threats relies on a proprietary process called Quantum L.E.A.P.S. It's certainly not a one-size-fits-all approach, but rather an eight-to-twelve-week process that's customized for each organization's unique needs. The process begins with a full-day discovery session with senior business leaders, includes a series of critical questions, uses three creative exercises, and is fueled by the collective experience of senior strategists.

When leaders answer a series of questions—provocative, probing, direct questions—they can reveal an organization's greatest potential (or its greatest barriers). Getting leaders to talk openly about major issues is one of the biggest keys to a successful planning process. We'll get to some of the questions and exercises on the following pages.

In the meantime, here are the seven fundamental structural concepts to incorporate in your planning process to help you and your team achieve an actionable outcome.

1. Involve All Decision Makers

Gathering the entire senior management team (even via video-conference or conference call) helps you to discuss issues holistically and eliminates the "silo" approach that's counter-productive to team building and breakthrough thinking. One of the most important features of this approach is that everyone hears the same thing at the same time. How participants internalize what they hear may differ, but all decision makers receive an equal opportunity to listen, speak, and make some preliminary decisions on key issues. Like a wedding, productive planning sessions adhere to a "speak now or forever hold your peace" set of guidelines.

2. Encourage "Possibility Thinking"

At this point in the process, there should be no "bad" ideas. Seek opportunities. Imagine possibilities. Avoid constraints. Opportunities, fresh perspectives, and new solutions emerge when constraints are suspended. Encourage multiple solutions. When you think you've got enough solutions, find ten more—most innovation occurs when there are at least ten options to consider.

3. Set Concrete Objectives

An objective is a dream with a deadline. Make sure the objective is achievable, measurable, and includes a deadline. Whether it's accelerating growth through a new product offering or resolving a customer retention issue, the team's goal must be clear. One component of setting objectives is to consider (and eventually analyze) what we call the "gold standards" of other organizations inside and outside your industry. "Gold standards" are those practices, leadership qualities, and business models that define the concept of excellence in the eyes of the marketplace. Your planning team should be able to ask and (eventually) answer questions that include: *What do the best companies do? How do they do it? Why do they do it this way? Why can't we? What can we learn from the successes and failures of others?*

4. Assess Reality

Make sure you're addressing the real issue. Then give your dream a reality test. Poke holes in positions. Ask, "Is this real? Can we win? Is it worth it?" Encourage all team members to challenge the thinking. By challenging the idea, one of two things will happen. Either the idea will be shown to be unworkable, or possible solutions to the challenges will emerge. Having previously suspended constraints, now is the time to gather and study internal data, industry trends, and marketplace developments to determine where opportunities and difficulties lie. This is the stage at which an organization's value proposition is tested, competitive advantage is affirmed, new strategies crystallize, and fresh solutions take shape. We often call this step "surgery without anesthesia." The assessment can be a painful dose of reality, but it's better to get the facts out in the open sooner rather than later. More on the topic of assessment and analysis in chapter 12.

5. Gain Agreement

Throughout the planning process, work diligently to ensure that senior leaders are aligned philosophically, strategically, financially, and operationally. It will be hard to develop a plan and budget (much less achieve the objective) if everyone's not on board. And if the senior leaders aren't on board, don't expect the rest of the organization to follow along. All differences must be resolved during the planning process. Implicit disagreements cannot be ignored. In working with large groups of leaders, achieving consensus can be hard work. But it's vital. "People will support what they have had a voice in deciding," says my friend Richard Hearne, whose consulting firm advises churches that are looking for ways to increase membership and congregational giving. Gaining agreement on problem definition and resolution is one of the two most important deliverables to emerge from any planning process.

6. Develop a Roadmap

A written plan is the second important deliverable. A written plan that is used throughout the year—and not thrown on the shelf as soon as it's been prepared—increases the odds of success. The plan must pinpoint priorities, action items, timing, responsibilities, resource commitments, milestones, and specific outcomes. Remember to build in opportunities for failure since failure is part of the process that ultimately helps lead to success.

7. Follow Through

An idea without execution is just an opinion. And a plan without action is a decision to do nothing, which is bad for morale. We'll examine ways to drive implementation and achieve accountability in chapters 14 and 27.

● ● ●

Organize your planning process around an initial meeting in which all participants are asked a series of questions. Here are six deceptively simple but powerful ones that will help you and your team take another step toward unlocking your company's competitive advantage and its full potential:

1. What Do You Want to Celebrate One Year from Today?

The difference between talking about "objectives" and making plans for a "celebration" changes the mindset of participants. In this particular exercise, the senior-most leader should always speak last in order to give others an opportunity to articulate their objectives, hopes, and dreams, which also helps gauge the extent to which everyone is or is not on the same page. How do your goals compare with other organizations that are considered the best at what they do? How do your plans compare with those organizations that have faced similar situations? "There is an infinite capacity to improve upon everything you do," says Bob Nardelli, chief executive of Home Depot. There are nuggets of new opportunity embedded in all organizations. A well-designed and well-run planning process will help dig them out.

2. How Would You Describe the Company Today?

A follow-up question, *"How would your customers describe the com-pany today?"* often reveals gaps between what the participants consider the company's current situation and where it needs to be to meet customer expectations. As outsiders working inside organizations, we at Bustin & Co. spend about 40 percent of our time probing in this area. It's interesting to listen to the answers of participants. Based on answers we've gotten in the past to our questions, we've wondered if all the participants were describing the same company. One of the tools we use to help illuminate the company's perceived marketplace position is called a Positioning Portrait [sm] (see diagram on next page). Before we can determine what its customers think of it, this exercise helps bring a new per-spective to how an organization views itself.

3. How Does Your Operation Bring Value to Customers?

Your customers, after all, ultimately define market leadership. Although historical performance is part of the equation, most of a company's value is tied to its future performance. Achieving optimal performance requires a plan and the commitment to execute the plan. Leaders must wed their vision to a bold yet practical strategy.

For any strategy to be successful, companies must under-stand the value of what they're selling. To help gain an internal perspective of where a company believes it provides value, we use a tool called the Value Revelation Chain[sm] (see page 100). This tool links the ways an organization touches customers, thereby revealing the value (if any) of these processes to the customer and, ultimately, to the organization.

To shape objectives and strategies and to determine the value of your company's products or services requires research, guided by questions such as:

Positioning Portrait℠

BUSTIN & CO.

Symbols, shapes, images and concepts that describe what the organization does and how others view it.

These images can include those in use now (i.e., logos and symbols) and those to be considered for future use.

Symbols

Personality

What are the animate qualities of your organization?

If your organization was a person, who would it be? Why?

What images come to mind when those inside your organization think about it?

What images come to mind when those outside the organization think about it?

Colors

Colors that may already be in use in logo, website, letterhead, office décor, etc.

Colors reflecting the organization's personality.

Sounds

Sounds that describe your organization.

These sounds can include words or phrases that are often heard as well as sounds that you associate with your organization (e.g., whooping it up when an achievement occurs).

Slogans

Slogans, phrases and words that describe your organization.

These words can include advertising headlines or taglines.

These words can also include words or phrases that are in common use or that are being used by other companies.

Situation

Where are your products or services found?

In what situations are your products or services used?

Are there other situations where they are not currently found or used but could be found or used in the future?

Product

All of the products and services currently provided by your organization.

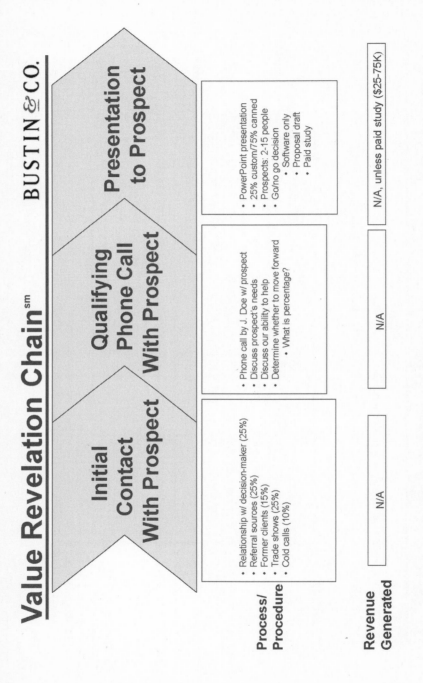

Value Revelation Chain℠

BUSTIN & CO.

Initial Contact With Prospect	Qualifying Phone Call With Prospect	Presentation to Prospect

Process/ Procedure

- Relationship w/ decision-maker (25%)
- Referral sources (25%)
- Former clients (15%)
- Trade shows (25%)
- Cold calls (10%)

- Phone call by J. Doe w/ prospect
- Discuss prospect's needs
- Discuss our ability to help
- Determine whether to move forward
  - What is percentage?

- PowerPoint presentation
- 25% custom/75% canned
- Prospects: 2-15 people
- Go/no go decision
  - Software only
  - Proposal draft
  - Paid study

Revenue Generated

N/A	N/A	N/A, unless paid study ($25-75K)

NOTE: This chart is the first of three produced during a strategic planning exercise, though the names and figures are fictional.

- What do customers and prospects like most and least about your company?
- What are the barriers customers and prospects must overcome to take the action we desire?
- What reward can we provide them for taking the action we desire?

While market research can be expensive, the most expensive research is none.

4. What Keeps You up at Night?

By understanding your customers, drilling down on the competition, thinking through scenarios outside your control that could make your business plan obsolete, and exploring your own weaknesses, you can begin to reformulate your strategy, fine-tune the one you've got, or plan a series of new initiatives to take advantage of your strengths and minimize your weaknesses.

5. What Would You Like Your Company to Achieve?

Seize the opportunity to cast aside barriers (at least for the moment) and think big. Again, the research will help guide what's possible and what's impractical.

6. What Changes Are You Committed to Making?

With this question we close our initial discovery session. We want to know right then what's up for grabs and what's a sacred cow. We also want to see whether the group is prepared to knuckle down for the hard work of implementation or ready to go back to business as usual.

● ● ●

Knowing which questions to ask is important. Knowing how to turn your answers into the sustainable, profitable growth you seek is where the real work begins.

"One question: If this is the Information Age, how come nobody knows anything?"

12

Making the Right Call
Using Knowledge to Drive Action

As you move through the planning process and come to the assessment and analysis phase, you and your team must gather and study data inside and outside the company in order to determine how best to keep your customers satisfied while meeting your profit targets.

These can be tough calls to make.

Late in the 2002 AFC divisional playoff game between Oakland and New England, Patriots quarterback Tom Brady cocked his arm to pass, was hit, and lost the ball. The referee ruled the play an incomplete pass. It was a crucial call in a critical part of the game. Interviewed after the game, the NFL's senior director of officiating Jerry Seeman said the rules were very clear and that the call was correct. "Each decision has two phases: you read and analyze the play, and then you make the call," Seeman said. "Those are the calls we love to make."

The rules for decision-making in business can also be very clear. Often, however, they are not.

You can achieve clarity by asking and answering three deceptively simple questions to support effective decision-making: Is the threat or opportunity real? Can we win? Is winning worth it?

Is it Real?

Having articulated clear, measurable objectives, ask, "How does pursuing an opportunity or fighting the battle support our strategic direction? Will the outcome benefit customers, employees, investors, and other stakeholders?" If the answer to either question is "no," you should abandon the idea.

Let's assume the answer is "yes." For the sake of this chapter, we've also assumed that you face an opportunity and not a threat, though the process for working through the analysis of a response to a perceived threat follows the same steps. (Addressing crises and threats will be examined in chapters 23–26.)

The question "Is it real?" leads to other considerations. Here are three steps to take to help answer that question:

1. Was the opportunity raised through a customer feedback process? Customers are great at telling you what they like and dislike.

2. What marketplace trends have you observed? Are others offering this product or service? Gather data, analyze trends, and draw initial conclusions.

3. Does the analysis indicate there's an emerging market? Test the opportunity with outside advisors.

It's worth spending some time at this juncture to dip into the world of competitive intelligence (CI). What you might not realize is that fully three-quarters of the information you need to understand your competitors is publicly available. Yet according to a market study by Knowledge Systems & Research, 87 percent of business leaders consider gathering intelligence information to support decisions and to develop and maintain winning strategies a major challenge.[68]

Your competitors generate enormous amounts of information that can be helpful to you in understanding your competitive environment. This information can come from your competitors' web sites, from their annual or company reports, government filings, and other public domain sources. Literature searches of published sources, including newspaper articles and trade publications, also are valuable. Noncompetitive sources such as industry experts, suppliers, financial analysts, and academics will account for the remaining 20 percent of your intelligence gathering.

CI is a systematic program for gathering and analyzing information about your competitors' activities and general business trends to accelerate your own business objectives. Whatever the size of your business, you'll outpace your competitors if you 1) understand how CI impacts your business; 2) know how to acquire the most helpful information; and 3) know how to use the information you acquire.

Any company battling for customers in a crowded market can benefit from CI. Smart companies realize that gathering, analyzing, and acting on intelligence about competitors, regulators, and customer issues can help them determine pricing, expansion opportunities, the types of products and services customers want, and the best time to introduce them. CI will also help identify the most likely candidates for alliances, acquisitions, or mergers.

But knowing how to sort the "need to know" from the "nice to know" requires significant experience.

Many of the functions that should be part of a CI initiative may already exist in your company in one shape or form. By themselves, they do not fully leverage an organization's competitive assets. But they certainly can offer information and insight, support a structured CI program, and use it to develop synergy. These existing resources include:

- Market research
- Customer analysis
- Strategic planning
- Financial benchmarks
- Information systems

Integrating these functions, departments, and resources will help you identify the remaining gaps in your intelligence-gathering capability.

The amount of time spent on gathering data should be about 25 percent of the CI process. That's because CI adds value to information gathering and strategic planning by introducing a disciplined system that not only *collects* information, but also analyzes it, disseminates findings, and forecasts outcomes based on that information. You can't make good decisions based only on *information*, no matter how accurate or comprehensive the information. What is needed is *intelligence*—the collection of information pieces that has been filtered, distilled, analyzed, and ultimately turned into strategy that can guide action.

Here are six simple yet effective ways to begin gathering important information about your current competitive environment—and helping you answer the question "Is it real"—using information that's all around you:

1. *Trade Shows*—These put your finger on the pulse of your industry. Show programs or catalogs from the top three shows in your field will list exhibitors with brief narrative copy for each. Many companies use these listings to announce new products, acquisitions, etc. The catalogs may also include advertising, seminar topics, sponsorships, press conference announcements, new initiatives, and bios of guest speakers.

    Where to go: www2.tsnn.com

    Cost: Information via Internet is free; trade show fees and catalog prices vary.

2. *Associations and Organizations*—As a member of your industry's largest trade association, you may have access to the member list, which not only lists your existing competitors, but also identifies upcoming competitors not currently on your radar screen. Associations can provide useful information about market trends, insights into maintaining your competitive edge, and new products or services.

    Where to go: www.associationcentral.com; info.asaenet.org/gateway/OnlineAssocSlist.html

    Cost: Websites are free; association membership fees vary.

3. *Patents and Trademark Records*—Monitoring your competitors' research activities is inexpensive, but can be time-consuming. It's relatively easy to access information

domestically and internationally about patent applications, branding changes in existing products or services, and new naming strategies.

Where to go: www.uspto.gov; www.delphion.com

Cost: Free.

4. *Chat Rooms*—Sponsor a chat room to encourage discussion of industry topics, or join a chat room to start such conversations. From Kraft Foods and The Coca-Cola Co. to Motorola and Stonyfield Farm, companies both large and small are fostering conversations on the web—and monitoring them—for half the cost of traditional research.

    Where to go: Association and organization web sites; web development firms

    Cost: Free to join a chat room; creating your own will vary with your needs.

5. *News Articles and Press Releases*—Business leaders tend to share more information about their company's strategy and vision during an interview than in sterilized press releases. Look for articles and mentions in newspapers and business or industry publications. Read news releases on your competitors' websites. Are they hiring senior level or highly technical people in an area that could reveal strategies not yet announced?

    Where to go: www.newsdirectory.com; www.publist.com, www.newslink.org

    Cost: Free.

6. *Employees*—Your own employees are the soldiers in the trenches, close to the battle, the ones who used to work for your competitors, and whose networks include contacts at those companies. They know what's selling, what's working, what isn't, and why. Harvest their knowledge with simple surveys through e-mail or interoffice mail.

Caution: The network works both ways; clearly explain your privacy and trade secrets policies to everyone.

Cost: Your time to create and tabulate the results and maybe some printing costs.

Information from these six sources will give you a basic understanding of the competitive environment in which you're operating. You don't need a sophisticated CI department to get started. But by transforming information you gather about other businesses into competitive intelligence, you will be better equipped to answer the question, "Is it real?"

Can We Win?

The second key question is not simply a numbers exercise, though the financial implications play a significant role in this process. This step focuses on the company's ability to align the opportunity and vision with the hard work of implementation.

You must ask yourself if you and your organization have the skill, experience, time, drive, and money to pursue the opportunity and succeed. Consider these four steps to help answer the "Can we win?" question:

1. View the situation from the outside in (more on this topic in chapter 20)

2. Identify all key issues and concerns

3. Revisit the "Is it real?" answer to determine what outcome is acceptable

4. Identify possible new options that may help you achieve your desired outcome

We use a chart that tracks the market lifecycle of products has stood the test of time through boom, bust, and back again. It's been a great barometer of performance and trends for packaged goods and manufactured products, as well as for a variety of service companies. We apply this chart to a range of financial and go-to-market scenarios as we examine clients' prospects for future success.

After the financial and go-to-market scenarios are fixed on the chart, we next overlay onto it competitive information that is gathered in the "*Is it real?*" analysis. Taken together, the two sets of data shown on the charts show—usually very clearly—whether it's possible for a company to win a particular market-share battle based on its product, its go-to-market strategy, and its marketplace position relative to its competition.

Is Winning Worth It?

So you've determined the opportunity is real and that winning is possible. Now comes the toughest question. Is winning worth it? This is the time to be pragmatic and committed. Winning requires commitment, and commitment always carries a cost. It's been said the difference between "involvement" and "commitment" is like a bacon-and-eggs breakfast: the chicken was "involved" but the pig was "committed."

A manufacturer that we advised over an extended period of time, for example, answered "yes" to the first two questions and then examined the cost of winning by analyzing several key areas.

- How would the new product affect the company's engineering department?
- Would the product's introduction negatively impact other products in the pipeline?
- Would adding this product be a burden to the sales force?

In this case, the benefits associated with the new product outweighed the risks. As a result, the product was introduced to industry acclaim with sales that achieved the financial success forecasted.

Making the right call is not always easy. But when your organization faces a key decision, ask—and answer—three fundamental questions to help drive the necessary action: *Is it real? Can we win? Is winning worth it?*

13

Branding
When Plans Become Promises

Having fine-tuned your value proposition with a written action plan, it's time to translate your competitive advantage into benefits for your organization's stakeholders. Now you must express your organization's aspirations, standards, and commitment through a brand: the delivery mechanism for communicating your intentions.

Business leaders speak warmly of their brands and programs developed to promote their brands. Ever wonder how many leaders use these terms without fully realizing the commitment their words—and their brands—imply? A brand, after all, is much more than a name, a logo, or a look. It's more than a trademark, clever packaging, or even a program. *A brand is all about making and keeping promises.*

Brands have existed for ages. Thousands of years ago, a Chinese emperor affixed his personal seal to important documents as evidence of his bond. In the Middle Ages, a knight carried a shield with a coat of arms identifying himself. An early American cattle rancher used a hot iron to mark (or brand) cattle as his property, and that mark—like imperial seals and coats of arms—grew to identify the rancher and became a symbol of his reputation.

Let's look at the key issues surrounding the purpose, development, and maintenance of a brand today.

The Value of a Brand

At last count, there were more than 1.2 million trademarks registered with the US government; millions more names and logos are registered with other governments worldwide. But names in and of themselves are not brands—they are identifiers. Brands have equity and value based on the associations important groups bring to them and the impact those associations have on behavior, particularly selection.

How much is a brand worth? *Business Week* reported that "brands aren't usually listed on corporate balance sheets, but they can go further in determining a company's success than a new factory or technological breakthrough . . . because nurturing a strong brand, even in bad times, can allow companies to command premium prices."[69]

According to J.P. Morgan Chase and Interbrand, the world's top ten brands—Coca-Cola, Microsoft, IBM, GE, Intel, Nokia, Disney, McDonald's, Marlboro and Mercedes—had a total market value in 2002 of $387.8 billion. Coca-Cola topped the list at $69.6 billion, and Mercedes rounded it out with a brand valued at $21 billion.[70]

Coca-Cola's chief executive once said that if forced to choose between the company's brand and everything else (including the secret formula, locked in an Atlanta vault), he'd take the brand. It stands to reason, then, that company leaders should take responsibility for identifying, articulating, and then cultivating their brand's essence, since doing so ultimately forms the basis of their organization's competitive advantage. It's good business. Consider these other examples.

Exxon and Mobil executives concluded that their two brands were so valuable they'd keep both after merging, lest they risk losing millions of customers—and dollars. Who says all gasoline is the same? That's the power of a brand.

Conversely, AOL Time Warner announced in September 2003 that it would drop "AOL" from its name, reverting to Time

Warner. Why? According to an internal memo, the move will eliminate "any confusion between our corporate name and the America Online brand name."[71] But perhaps what's at the heart of the "confusion" is the belief from inside and outside the organization that the one entity was tarnishing the reputation of the other. AOL was seen by some as a staggering example of the "irrational exuberance" of the dot-com era—complete with an equally exuberant purchase price that has a long, long way to go before Time Warner shareholders see any value. Meanwhile, AOL proponents pointed to the fact that Time Warner is navigating its way through SEC and Justice Department investigations for accounting irregularities, moves that are not well received by Wall Street and customers.[72]

Three manufacturers in the crowded upscale car market use their brands' promises of a unique experience to differentiate themselves. Mercedes promises prestige, Lexus luxury, Volvo safety.

Wal-Mart is expanding its promise of a limited selection of inexpensively priced products into its new Neighborhood Markets grocery stores. Can Wal-Mart keep this promise? Absolutely. Whole Foods Market—jumping to thirty-second from forty-eighth on *Fortune's* 2003 list of most admired companies—promises fresh, organic meat, fish, produce, and cheeses. That's its essence. What is Safeway's essence? We couldn't tell you—and that's a problem for that brand as the company continues to lose market value (up to $20 billion in shareholder wealth in the last three years) and top executive talent (four senior executives have departed in the period December 2002 through January 2003).[73]

Developing and Maintaining Your Brand

To consider what it takes to develop, update, or maintain a brand, we will rewind twenty-four hundred years.

Remember that in chapter 5 we said leaders wrestling with change must follow the lead of Greek philosopher Socrates, who believed that deep within everything concrete resides the idea of the thing itself, or its essence. "Know thyself," Socrates said. Just as you must know your strengths and weaknesses as a leader, you must also know—and ultimately codify—the strengths and weaknesses of your organization. Remember that Socrates believed that self-knowledge is the starting point, because the greatest source of confusion is the failure to realize how little we know about anything, including ourselves.

Borrow from Socrates' method of approaching subjects in a question-the-premise style that helps you and your leadership team assimilate facts, eliminate conflicting data, and draw conclusions. As noted in chapter 11, the Positioning Portrait^{sm} helps you separate where you are (your position) from where you want to be (your positioning statement). Completing this exercise helps bring new perspectives to bear on an organization's corporate personality, its products, how the marketplace values those products, and the promise an organization is willing to make to its stakeholders.

It's critical for an organization to find its intrinsic competitive advantage and leverage it. That advantage can be expressed as a "positioning statement" that reflects the essence of why an organization, its products, or its services exists.

As you think about positioning—or repositioning—your organization, product or service, be sure to apply these four critical tests. Your position must:

- Reflect values you hold dear
- Be clear and relevant in the minds of your stakeholders
- Be singular—you cannot be all things to all people
- Set you apart—it must be distinctive and compelling

Just one of these characteristics is not enough. To be powerful, a positioning statement must meet each of these four tests.

The chart below depicts the role and power of a compelling positioning statement. Notice how all forms of an organization's methods for connecting with their stakeholders cascade from the positioning statement.

BUSTIN &CO.

Winning hearts and minds

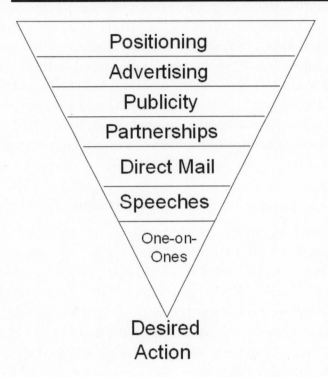

Positioning

Advertising

Publicity

Partnerships

Direct Mail

Speeches

One-on-
Ones

Desired
Action

Baylor Law School, a program ranked consistently in the top twenty-five among all US law schools, concluded that its current facilities were not commensurate with the quality of education it provided. Dean Brad Toben and his advisors began planning for a new campus. They retained a noted architectural firm and set the funding target at $27.5 million. The alumni base of approximately five thousand lawyers was fairly evenly distributed among defense and plaintiff attorneys, who typically do not view one another favorably, and this presented a challenge. The school also desired to reduce enrollment and increase the quality of applications, though its recruiting methods had changed little over time. Baylor Law School retained Bustin & Co., and following in-depth meetings and a thorough analysis of the school's financial and historical records and external competitive data, we worked together to develop a two-pronged strategy designed to achieve the school's objectives: 1) strengthen the school's national reputation; 2) attract high-quality students while retaining the excellent faculty members. A positioning statement was developed to capture the essence of Baylor Law School, what it strives to accomplish daily, and what it would become in the future. In order to challenge the alumni to give liberally, the positioning statement needed to encompass the school's competitive advantage and to aspire to future greatness.

Baylor Law School is the best in the country at teaching students how to be functional, practicing attorneys.

This statement drove all content and design of the capital campaign, especially stimulating and attracting major gifts from alumni. At the completion of this campaign, Baylor opened its new law school for the fall semester of 2001. The school had raised $40 million, a 69 percent increase over the original $27.5 million target. Quality of student applicants had risen by 25 percent based on LSAT scores. Moreover, the process did not alienate a single influential alumnus. The ability to reduce to a single sentence the facts, memories, and dreams of an institution and its alumni helped propel the campaign to heights not previously considered attainable.

What's critical to remember is that if your brand's promise is not supported by performance, promotional efforts actually erode your brand's value. For that reason, employees are a crucial link to your other constituents. When employees understand and reflect the core brand values, they radiate out to customers and other stakeholders.

Russ Klein is a savvy marketer and terrific leader, and I've been privileged to work with him when he held the top marketing post at The Seven-Up Company and again, most recently, in his current position as chief marketing officer at Burger King Corporation.

Klein has a provocative way of describing the challenge mature brands face when they are trying to change stakeholders' perceptions of past performance and reconnect with them. "When they know you more than love you," he says, "you must find a way to infuse your brand with some mystique that will draw people back to you." He calls this approach "shattering knowledge"— a move designed to reset performance expectations.

In the case of virtually all successful companies, performance more than matches the promotion.

Brands must keep their promise. Failure to do so, to paraphrase Jung, means the decline and eventual journey down the road to perdition for the product, service, or enterprise.

14

Turning Plans into Profits

Apositioning statement will not execute itself. Left unattended, it will have no more influence on behavior than the typical New Year's resolution. By taking certain steps during and immediately following any planning or goal-setting process, you increase the odds that you will achieve your objectives. To avoid the trap of implementing unproductive "conscience-easing activities," sharpen your goals by developing these habits of excellence:

- Live in the now
- Be clear about what you want
- Execute the plan

Live in the Now

Have you ever wondered what your most precious commodity is? It's time. Because once you lose it you'll never get it back.

Goals, of course, are about the future. But to set and achieve goals you must first understand, embrace, and realize the power of the present. Most people fail to achieve their goals due to their failure to live in the "now." People that live in the now unleash the power of the present. Larry Mahan, an icon in competitive rodeos, echoes these sentiments as he compares horses and people. "Horses live in the moment," Mahan says. "Our mind, body and spirit have control, but we never live in the moment. We think too often about yesterday or tomorrow."[74] As he instructs people on horse riding, he says "we try to teach people to be in total control of their energy, and the horses help. A horse will let you know if you're stressed by the way it reacts to you. It will be a reflection of your energy level."[75]

Living in the now is necessary because the past is over—you can't change it. The future is uncertain—you can't foresee it. The past and the future are illusions. We have only the present within our grasp and, God willing, it's the closest thing under our control.

By focusing on the present, you commit yourself to change and to success. This attitude embraces the idea that if you act today and do the things that you commit to doing, you can succeed.

But annual plans dissolve when:

- Goals are abstract
- You live in the past and dream in the future
- You don't set your attitude to make the required changes
- You don't see that what you're doing today makes a difference toward achieving your goal

These thoughts and others like them are nothing but excuses.

Be Clear about What You Want

Clarity is the second point of the three-point goal-setting plan, and there are three components to the discipline of clarity: Being very specific about what you want, setting a deadline, and writing it down.

Be Specific

Wanting to lose weight is a dream; losing ten pounds by Labor Day is specific. Wanting to be rich is a dream; increasing your income by 30 percent by Christmas is specific.

Set a Deadline

Assigning a deadline to a specific goal makes the goal more attainable. Deadlines are powerful tools. As noted in chapter 11, start your planning process by asking: *What do you want to celebrate one year from today?* Because if you don't achieve your twelve-month objectives, you can forget about your three- and five-year plans. It's healthy to dream, and you need to leave room for that in the planning process, but once you reach the implementation phase, you and your team must focus on achieving specific, concrete, doable, measurable goals.

Write It Down

Committing goals to paper (or disc) preserves your thinking and forces you to measure progress. Saying it isn't enough; writing down goals requires discipline and increases the chances of success. *What are we doing? Why? Who's doing it? By when? At what cost? For what expected result?*

Three of the most successful business leaders of all time know the importance of committing goals to paper. Stephen Covey uses a four-box quadrant in which he places activities that are urgent but not important, urgent and important, not urgent and not important, and not urgent but important.[76]

Southwest Airlines Chairman Herb Kelleher makes two columns—one that reads, "Must be completed today" and the other that reads, "Can be completed tomorrow."[77]

Andrew Carnegie favored an even simpler approach. My friend John Dealey tells of Carnegie's desire in the early 1900s to harness the benefits of time management. Carnegie retained a consultant to develop an easy-to-use system that would deliver a huge impact. The system consisted of three simple components:

1. At the start of each day, make a list of tasks to complete

2. Mark six items considered most important at that time

3. Work on the single item, or part of that item, that is the most important at that moment until it is completed or something else becomes more important

Look simple? Try it.

Execute the Plan

Here are six keys to executing your plan:

1. *Limit yourself to three goals.* When you achieve those goals, set three more. Trying to solve more than three goals or objectives at a time will only dilute your efforts. Stay focused.

2. *Commit to improvement.* Ferry Porsche believes "Change is easy, but improvement is far more difficult." You must make a decision to stick with it.

3. *Display your goals.* Carry your goals in your pocket or make them a screen saver. Look at them every day. By keeping your goals before you, you cannot misplace your most important priorities.

4. *Act today; do not procrastinate.* Why put off what you can do today? Make each day count. Holiday Inn founder Kemmon Wilson says, "You cannot procrastinate—in two days, tomorrow will be yesterday." Remember that once time is gone it cannot be recovered.

5. *Hold yourself accountable.* You have adopted an attitude of change. Your list keeps you focused. If necessary, a partner can get you back on track. Review your objectives and reset them if you must, but don't give up. Honor your commitments to achieve the goal you have set.

6. *Celebrate victories.* In uncertain times, celebrations are more important than ever. So take time to savor your accomplishments and to reward and recognize those who have played a part in achieving success. Most professional athletes adopt a "twenty-four-hour rule" following a game. That is, they have twenty-four hours to savor the victory before moving on. Conversely, they also forget about losses and look to the future once the twenty-four-hour period has passed. Enjoy, at least for a brief period, your accomplishments. Celebrating victories provides an opportunity to look at the progress that's been made—and provides a context for continuing the journey toward the objective.

Unlock the following anonymous riddle—and your success—using the keys provided thus far:

> I am your constant companion. I am your greatest helper or heaviest burden. I will push you onward or drag you down to failure. I am completely at your command. Half the things you do might just as well be turned over to me, and I will be able to do them quickly and correctly.
>
> I am easily managed—you must merely be firm with me. Show me exactly how you want something done and after a few lessons I will do it automatically. I am the servant of all great people; and, alas, of all failures as well. Those who are great, I have made great. Those who are failures, I have made failures.
>
> I am not a machine, though I work with all the precision of a machine plus the intelligence of a human being. You may run me for profit or turn me for ruin—it makes no difference to me.
>
> Take me, train me, be firm with me and I will place the world at your feet. Be easy with me and I will destroy you.
>
> Who am I? I am habit.

As Aristotle said, "We are what we repeatedly do. Excellence, then, is not an act but a habit."

Part 4

Guidelines for Changing Companies

"It happened either over the weekend or when I left the office today for lunch."

15

Butch Cassidy's Rules for a Knife Fight

In the movie *Butch Cassidy and the Sundance Kid*, there's a scene in which Butch and Sundance return to their hideout, and one of the outlaws challenges Butch's leadership. Butch reminds the gang that his planning and implementation have produced results. He says the business of robbery has become more complicated and dangerous and that he is best qualified to lead the group through these changing times. The men are not persuaded, and they propose a fight to the death between Butch and his challenger. Before the fight, Butch says he wants to establish the rules. The challenger relaxes. "Rules in a knife fight?" he asks. Butch seizes the moment to sucker-punch his challenger, win the fight, and restore his leadership position.

Ever felt like Butch? Not that you'd ever deliver a sucker punch.

But have you ever felt your ability to handle change effectively has diminished? That you're continually fighting to stay on top or to get back on top? Maybe you're fighting an operational battle to increase productivity and profits. Perhaps you're trying to convince your board to commit more R&D funds to enhance a product to help increase market share. You could be wrestling with the need to develop and implement a more compelling strategy on which to stake the company's future.

Whatever battle you may be fighting, follow twelve time-tested rules to capitalize on change.

12 Rules for Changing Companies

Over the years, our work with companies experiencing significant change has given us a distinctive position from which to
develop and then implement strategies, processes, and programs
to help leaders capitalize on change. These rules articulate a set of
guidelines we have watched successful organizations follow and
less successful organizations miss.

1. You Have Only One Reputation

Thomas Paine observed, "Character is easier kept than recovered." Consider Martha Stewart's recent conviction over a questionable stock sale. Even before her case went to trial in 2004, her
company's stock lost more than 50 percent of its value. *Martha
Stewart Living* lost at least ten advertisers accounting for over a
million dollars in revenue in 2003.[78] Additionally, the magazine
lost half a million of its 2.3 million readers, which has forced it to
cut ad rates.[79] Before Stewart lost in a court of law, she lost in the
court of public opinion. In her attempt to save what amounted to
about $45,000 through her stock-dumping deal, her company's
market capitalization lost about a half-billion dollars, and she
spent some $400,000 *per month* to remake her image.[80] All this,
however, will not restore her reputation and she'll never be able
to lead a public company.

2. Know Who You Are and Where You're Going

Prepare a written plan with specific, measurable objectives the
entire company understands, embraces, and follows. Use the
approaches, exercises, and tools found in chapter 11. Kmart
could not figure out what it stood for or where it was going. In
the late 1990s, Kmart's revenues flagged. In response, Kmart
defined its value proposition first against Sears, then against
Target, and finally against Wal-Mart. It wasted precious time
and money trying to reposition itself with each restage effort
and succeeded only in confusing the public. It achieved no marketplace traction, profitability, or sustainability before filing for
bankruptcy in 2002. Some blue light special.

3. Value Is Determined Outside Your Company

Identify your core competency, confirm the value the market places on it, and then differentiate yourself from those offering similar products or services. If you can't answer "Why us?" don't expect the market to know. Once you've uncovered your competitive advantage through the planning and research process, leverage it. Southwest Airlines translates its value to "everyday low fares." So while most airlines have used the impact of the September 11 terrorist attacks, soaring fuel costs, and decreased travel to explain decreased revenue and profits are down, Southwest Airlines continues to report record earnings in the same market, same industry, same time frame. But they achieve different results based on a near-flawless execution of a strategy that gives customers more of what they value.

4. Stay Focused

Follow Covey's "End in mind" principle,[81] and remember that distractions pull you away from your objectives. Nicky Otts, chief executive of Recept Rx, a very profitable holding company that operates pharmacies in several cities, identified an opportunity to acquire a healthcare company that he believed would add value to his core business. Otts retained our firm, and we conducted market research that supported Otts's belief that the acquisition could meet an underserved need and provide a better-than-average opportunity for success. Working together, we then developed a business plan that articulated the new company's competitive advantage and outlined an action plan. In 2001, Otts acquired the healthcare company, formed and launched a new company, and combined these two entities under his umbrella organization. Within twelve months, however, Otts concluded that the new venture was not complementary to his core business and, in fact, was draining significant management energy and hundreds of thousands of dollars. The problem was that the operating requirements to pursue this new market were quite different from those in his core business. The acquired company proved to be a huge distraction to the core business, which all the while continued to grow and generate substantial profits. Otts therefore made the tough but smart decision to cease operating the company he acquired and return his focus to his highly profitable core business. All signs point to the continued growth and success of Recept Rx, but it took a diversion to help Otts fully appreciate what he already had—and the benefits of focus.

5. You Can't Jump Half a Ditch

Remember the idea espoused by nineteenth-century Prussian general Karl von Clausewitz, who disagreed with the notion "that half efforts can be effective." Von Clausewitz went on to say that "no one wanting to cross a wide ditch would cross half of it first." Change is best addressed boldly, not sheepishly. After determining essential activities, do your best in every task, no matter how small. Small efforts add up, but half-hearted efforts are fatal.

6. If It's Worth Doing, It's Worth Measuring

Monitor and assess the effectiveness of all activities. How else will you replicate success and eliminate failure? "What gets measured gets done," says Bonnie Reitz, senior vice president for sales and distribution at Continental. "If it's worth doing, do it. We have 2,000 flights every day. All those accolades we got yesterday? Poof! They were yesterday. It's today, and we've got to do it again."[82] We'll examine the measurement process in greater detail in chapter 27.

7. Hire and Retain the Best; Terminate Underperformers

Employees and suppliers that embrace change and perform stay; those that don't must go. Average performance during times of change hobbles a company. Hold people accountable, starting with yourself. At Microsoft, the policy is to determine the criteria for the position, hire only the top 5 percent of candidates who are the smartest—not necessarily the most knowledgeable—for the job since knowledge can be acquired. The "secret," writes David Thielen in *The 12 Simple Secrets of Microsoft Management*, is to remember that "you are only as good as the people who report to you. The quality of your employees determines whether or not you can succeed. Do not compromise."[83] Wolfgang von Goethe said some two hundred years ago, "If my people fail, I cannot succeed. If my people succeed, I cannot fail." This idea remains true today.

8. Speed Is a Weapon; It Can Help and Hurt You

Speed can offer leaders and their companies a competitive advantage, particularly in times of change. The key is to realize that simply doing things quickly is no guarantee of success and can even backfire. Remember the so-called "first-mover advantage" of the dot-com era? Many companies were more concerned about being first than developing a profitable business model. "Fast is fine," said Wyatt Earp, "but accuracy is everything." That said, when you've gathered your facts, thought through your options and reached a decision, implement it quickly and move on.

9. If It Seems Too Good to Be True, It Probably Is

Most get-rich-quick schemes fail. Consider the tulip-mania of seventeenth-century Holland "when one fool hatched from another, the people were rich without substance and wise without knowledge."[84] Some tulip speculators got rich, but many lost their clogs. The same was true of the dot-com mania of the late 1990s. Hundreds of dot-com startups, having secured venture capital despite flawed business strategies, predictably failed because they defied the fundamentals of business—such as running operations in a sea of red ink. Successful enterprises leaven their optimism and data with proven experience and solid judgment.

10. Love Your Customers or Someone Else Will

Regularly ask your clients about their businesses, their dreams, their fears, their competition, and the job your company is doing for them. Respond accordingly. When you love your customers, you make it harder for your competition to gain a foothold. John Alexander, chief executive of Inventory Dynamics and a former Emery Air Freight executive, makes sure his clients know exactly what service he provides and what it costs. He told me that this prevents his clients from imagining that his extraordinary service is routine and therefore inexpensive. Neither side of a business relationship should attempt to take unfair advantage.

11. You Can't Save Your Way to Prosperity

Trying to grow by cutting budgets is like standing in a bucket and trying to raise yourself by the handle. While continued sales declines often necessitate cutting expenses and prices, remember to ask yourself, "What investments can we *not* afford to cut?" As Steve Jobs, cofounder and chief executive of Apple noted in a *New York Times* interview after delivering a quarterly earnings home run in the middle of a recession, "We had a lot of innovation this quarter, and our customers responded favorably."[85] Investing in your business—not cost-cutting—unlocks a company's value.

12. Never Give Up

"When you reach the end of your rope," said Franklin D. Roosevelt, "tie a knot and hang on." Roosevelt faced some of the toughest challenges any leader will ever confront: the Great Depression; mobilizing a reluctant nation in the face of Britain's request for supplies to battle Hitler; the attack on Pearl Harbor that propelled the country into World War II; and, of course, his personal battle with polio. Roosevelt not only hung on, he rallied others to the causes he believed in. There's always a way to move forward, so fight for your beliefs.

You've probably noticed that these twelve rules correspond in some ways to the nine character traits explored in chapter 7 that are critical for any leader who has wrestled with change and come out on top. It's no coincidence. The best rules for confronting change arise from personal attributes and beliefs that translate into smart ways of doing business that never change. How to apply these rules may change and evolve with the times, but they remain fundamentally the same from century to century.

Knowing the rules helped Butch Cassidy to overcome adversity and questions about his leadership. These twelve can help you.

"Won't all these new rules impact adversely on the viability of small businesses with fewer than fifty employees?"

16

An Entrepreneur's Ten Commandments

The US Bureau of Labor estimates that about 95 percent of American businesses are small and mid-size companies—entrepreneurial enterprises.

Even if you're not an entrepreneur, this chapter can offer perspective you may find helpful, because the best big companies work diligently to continue operating their businesses like the startups they once were in order to stay close to their customers, retain their edge, and keep their people motivated. Moreover, many senior executives have been displaced by the recent economic downturn. Unable to find suitable positions with companies—or perhaps unwilling to work for anyone but themselves the next time around—they are starting new businesses.

So whether you're starting a business, or you're a seasoned entrepreneur who has survived the odds showing most new companies fail within the first two years, there are guidelines that can accelerate your success and help you to avoid the crippling mistakes associated with change, uncertainty, and new beginnings. Although the rules for successful entrepreneurs and leaders in larger organizations are similar, there are some significant differences. Leading a small business versus a large one is like the difference between driving a sports car and a luxury car: the thrills are greater, but you also feel more of the road's bumps.

More Than a Good Idea and Money

Most entrepreneurs start their business with what they believe is a good idea but often don't understand the market. Investors funding what appears on paper to be a good idea perpetuate the belief that a market exists for the idea. But we've all seen that a sustainable business takes more than a good idea and money. It takes passion, drive—oh, yes, and profitable customers.

"There is only one opportunity you should be thinking about," writes entrepreneur and author Norm Brodsky, "during the start-up of any business: Building a customer base that will make the business able to sustain itself on its own internally generated cash flow."[86]

Succeeding in uncertain times is difficult. Mistakes can sink a young company or a small company. And they can be absolutely devastating to a company that is both young and small.

At the end of a particularly difficult year, I was asking myself if I could have done things differently. What were some of the things I should've done that I didn't do? What did I do that I shouldn't have done? What would I do differently if I were just starting out?

After much reflection, I developed these Ten Commandments.

I then shared my thinking with Jerry White, director of the Caruth Institute for Entrepreneurship at SMU's Cox School of Business, who leads and teaches programs dedicated to helping business leaders understand and prepare for the demands of running a small business. White told me that the most common mistakes entrepreneurs make are 1) expanding too quickly; 2) assuming too much debt; and 3) taking customers for granted.

We agreed that another huge mistake is lack of goal alignment, and you'll see this thought echoed elsewhere in this book. Entrepreneurs, White and I agreed, that get lost in their "vision" may talk about the five-year goal while their people are thinking about 5 o'clock and getting the heck out of the place. Goal alignment means the goals of the entrepreneur and the goals of the employees are one and the same

An Entrepreneur's Ten Commandments

How can leaders of small and mid-sized companies succeed? These ten "commandments" can help entrepreneurs avoid costly mistakes and achieve profitablility. You'll see that they're similar in some respects to the rules for changing companies in the preceding chapter, but these "commandments" offer some unique guidelines for leaders of smaller companies.

1. Know Where You're Going

Whether you're a big company, a little company, or a startup, you must be very clear about your objective, identify your core competency, and then differentiate your organization from its competition. If you and your employees can't answer "why you?" neither will the marketplace, and you won't have any customers. You must know your goal and remain focused on it. Avoid the temptation to try to be too many things to too many people. John Dealey hosts a forum that brings owners of small businesses together on a regular basis to trade war stories, share insights, and offer support to one another. He regularly reminds entrepreneurs that "over the centuries, the accumulation of wealth has been driven by focus." This is one rule that, if not followed, will sink any company.

2. Cash Is King

Understand the difference between cash, profit, and revenue. If you don't, you probably won't make payroll. You can be extremely profitable (on paper) but still find yourself strapped for cash. Fast growth drains cash, and cash-flow problems can cause bad decisions. There is a reason cash is king. Don't learn why the hard way.

3. Customers First, Employees Second

Cash starts with customers, not employees. If you don't take care of your customers, someone else will. However, if you don't take care of your employees, someone else will. But you must put your customers first. You must impress upon your employees the imperative of customer service. Your employees' success depends upon your customers' satisfaction. Taking customers for granted will kill any company. "In the relentless pursuit of new business," says White, "it can be easy to assume that those who currently buy from you will continue to do so. In difficult economic environments, your competitors are hungry and will gladly serve the customer you underserve."

4. Drive Sales

"Everyone," says White, "must be involved in helping drive sales—from the chief executive to the administrative assistant to the accounting department. 'If you build it they will come' is baloney. If you build it and sell the heck out of it they may come," White told me.

5. Have a Great Banker and Line of Credit

Understand how much debt your company can handle. "Leverage is a two-edged sword," says White. "It's great in good times but is frequently the thing that kills a company in difficult times. I prefer debt-to-equity—that is, total liabilities divided by equity—to be 1.0 or less."

6. Work on the Business, Not Just in It

Spend one-third of your time with customers, one-third getting new customers, and one-third thinking strategically about the future. Dan Edelman founded in 1952 what has become the world's largest independent public relations firm. He reminds the leaders ·in his firm throughout the world to maintain this equilibrium. If your time is out of balance, chances are your business will be, too. Make sure you spend as much time *on* the business as you do *in* the business.

7. Install Systems

A company growing without systems and procedures is a time bomb waiting to explode. Our firm's lack of systems in the late 1990s severely impeded our productivity and decision-making abilities. We were so focused on riding the fast growth wave and serving clients that we regularly reinvented the wheel—on everything from organizing work teams to presenting our work to clients, billing for services, determining compensation, and tracking vacation time. Upon realizing this, we took weeks, and a few blunt conversations, to establish and then implement systems and procedures throughout the staff. Although it was neither a smooth nor pretty transition, it made us more productive both in serving our clients and in running our business.

8. Protect What's Yours

Retain a lawyer to safeguard names and ideas, structure employment forms, review transactions, and establish bylaws. Greg Carr, an intellectual property lawyer, told me that "as companies grow and become more successful, they can become targets of organizations with deep pockets that want to take advantage of smaller companies. Taking steps to protect your property is, unfortunately, often ignored by leaders," he says. Carr estimates that one-third of the entrepreneurs he's come into contact with either have not patented their intellectual property or have failed to register their trademarks. Do the things as a smaller company that big companies do.

9. Don't Give Away Equity

Few of us value free offers, because they come with strings at-
tached or have little value. So if you grant options or offer equity to
those you work with, be sure the recipients write checks or forego
raises or bonuses of significance when the transactions are completed, as a demonstration of the shares' value. When Dale Sellers,
chief executive of Phoenix 1 Restoration & Construction, asked his
so-called partners to share in the risks and sacrifices of ownership,
it became obvious they viewed the business arrangement as simply another mechanism for collecting bonuses. He made the tough
but correct decision to end these relationships. The result, he told
me, was surprisingly liberating and uplifting. "There's no doubt
that I miss their skills, but it's clear they weren't true partners—
they were just well compensated employees who weren't as committed to the business as I was. The remaining employees have
risen to the challenge, and I've enjoyed the opportunity to work
more directly with our clients and employees."

10. Persistence Pays

Jim Smith has led his CPA firm, Smith, Jackson, Boyer & Bovard,
through difficult times that would have claimed the organizations of lesser leaders. After completing their best year ever in
1985, Smith and his partners watched as the collapse of banking
and real estate caused their clients' businesses to fail at a rate of
one per week. One-sixth of the firm's total fee volume disap-
peared within six months, and a disgruntled client sued them for
$1.7 million in damages for work performed. Smith delivered the
grim news to his partners and employees. "There will be no
bonuses, no raises, but no layoffs," he told them. "But we must
find new business." By cutting costs, involving the entire organization in the new business effort, and forming a strategic alliance
with another firm to offset overhead, Smith rode out the storm.

By the end of 1988, the economy began to recover, and Smith's firm returned to profitability. Stay with it.

●   ●   ●

For entrepreneurs, following these Ten Commandments can transform a hellish business operation into one that's heavenly.

"My son, you have survived the ordeal by fire and the ordeal by water. You now face the final challenge—ordeal by media."

17

When Change Brings Conflict and Scrutiny

As a leader wrestling with change, sooner or later you'll probably find yourself talking with a reporter. Whether the conversation is the result of a change in management or strategy, the introduction of a new product, or the need to provide your perspective on layoffs or litigation, your time will come.

Here's why. The lines between public and private organizations are disappearing. Tom Leppert, chief executive of the $6.5 billion Turner Construction Co., says that

> the bifurcation between the public and private sectors has gone away. We used to once think of the public sector here and the private sector there, and never the two shall meet. That's simply not the case now. No matter what business you're in, you're in the public sector . . . We can see it in a whole host of situations where one crisis that was mishandled has arguably destroyed companies.[87]

Or as Abraham Lincoln said in 1869, "Public opinion in this country is everything."

When your time comes to talk will you be ready? Will you meet the press with confidence? Or will you approach this encounter with a bit of fear? Or—worse yet—will you simply try to avoid talking at all?

Why Talk at All?

Talking with reporters makes sense because the news media serve as gatekeepers to an organization's audience. You control your advertising but not news about your company, which is driven by events largely outside your control. Moreover, news has more credibility than ads. After all, we buy a newspaper to read the news, not the ads. Even cynics view reporters as third-party observers charged with presenting an issue fairly and accurately. So we look to the news media as reliable sources of information.

News, however, by definition concerns new developments. In other words, "business as usual" rarely makes news. Conflict, change, and uncertainty attract the attention of business reporters.

So why talk at all if we know reporters often look for conflict? There are two primary reasons. First, when your time comes and you duck the interview, the reporter will simply find other sources willing to talk. These sources can include unknowledgeable "experts," disgruntled former or current associates, and the competition. Second, an interview provides an opportunity for you to communicate your side of the story. When you approach an interview with preparation, and as an opportunity instead of a confrontation, you wield a powerful tool.

Ask Your Own Questions First

Someone has observed that the four worst words in the English language are, "'60 Minutes' is here."

Few leaders must prepare for the likes of "60 Minutes." Yet some of the organizations we've worked with have faced such situations, and even for that level of intense scrutiny we have recommended going ahead with the interview in order to set forth the organization's point of view.

When thinking through any interview, ask:

- Is now the best time to tell our story? If not, can we suggest another time?
- Is this the news outlet or reporter we want to tell our story?
- Who should speak for our organization?

- How will our key audiences react when they see or hear the story?
- What ancillary issues are likely to be raised that represent a downside for us?

You must analyze scenarios, approaches, and likely outcomes and proceed accordingly. Rarely should an organization avoid an interview—only when the story will present a "no-win" situation. An organization should respond to no-win circumstances with a written statement. And no matter how rude the reporter, don't lose your temper. Will Rogers observed that it's best to "avoid fighting with people who buy their ink by the gallon and paper by the ton."

You must also understand what an interview can and cannot do. At best, a well-conducted interview can help change public opinion, and ultimately behavior, about a person or issue. Well-considered comments provide another perspective that, when woven into the story by the reporter, provides a balanced account of an issue. Nonetheless, an interview cannot turn bad facts into good ones. Or, as Barbara Bower, a principal at Trammell Crow Company says, "You can't talk your way out of something you behaved your way into."

Be Prepared

Let's assume you accept the premise that it generally makes sense to talk to, rather than avoid, a reporter. We've already pointed out that if you fail to plan, you plan to fail. This promise applies to interviews.

The Fort Worth Zoo, the nation's third largest, has long been recognized as an innovator. In 2001, the zoo planned to launch a new exhibit called "Texas Wild!" that would showcase the flora and fauna of the Lone Star State. But the zoo faced criticism from animal advocates and media when it announced that the new exhibit would include a "hunting as conservation" theme. The controversy threatened to polarize donors, visitors and staff, limit donations to the $40 million capital campaign, and tarnish the zoo's reputation. Working with zoo leaders, we developed an educational campaign that highlighted the zoo's record of innovation, featured extensive research countering opponents' accusations, and promoted conservation messages, including hunting as a tool. We anticipated issues and prepared fact-based responses to advance the zoo's position and to balance or neutralize opponents' claims. The capital campaign raised $45 million, negative press was virtually non-existent, and the exhibit has continued to enjoy local and national acclaim.

Conversely, failure to prepare will lead to an unclear message, which in turn will result in a story about what the reporter thought you said, rather than what you said.

Here are five essentials for conducting smart interviews.

1. Understand the Agenda

An interview is a different kind of business meeting. You wouldn't think of going into a business meeting unprepared. So prepare for your meeting with the media.

2. Focus on Three Key Points

Most people can only remember three main thoughts in one setting. Identify your three, and stay "on message." It may seem boring, but it works. In the sound-bite world we live in, straying from your three key messages can spell trouble. Staying "on message" will help you to shape the story's headline. Imagine the headline.

3. Always Tell the Truth

If you doubt the wisdom of this, review the section on "Honesty" in chapter 7. Truthfulness is the right thing to do, it preserves your reputation, and as a practical matter, half-truths and lies have never been easier to detect with online resources.

4. Don't Repeat the Negative

Make your point, not the reporter's.

5. Everything Is "on the Record"

"Off the record" is for Hollywood. If you say it, be sure you'll be happy reading it in tomorrow's newspaper or seeing it on tonight's news. Otherwise, don't say it.

● ● ●

Get ready. Your fifteen minutes of fame could be right around the corner when you meet the press.

"*We study, we plan, we research. And yet, somehow, money still remains more of an art than a science.*"

18

The Difference
between Success and
Failure

A single silver bullet rarely will enable a company to profit from the uncertainties of change. Usually, a combination of factors leads to success or failure.

Here's a side-by-side comparison of two companies that highlights how different approaches to seven crucial steps made the difference between success and failure. Bustin & Co. worked with both companies, and we'll keep their identities confidential.

Company A was a fast-growing Fortune 500 healthcare services company that sought to refine and clarify its business direction in order to maximize shareholder value. The company's success was a result of the chief executive's vision driving an aggressive acquisition strategy to build critical mass. But the growth-by-acquisition approach was in danger of running out of steam. Changes in healthcare regulation and mounting price pressures threatened to erode the company's market position and depress its stock price. Furthermore, few people outside the top leader's inner circle understood where the company was headed, why it was headed there, or what was in it for them.

Company B, a mid-sized technology company operating as the US subsidiary of an international conglomerate, faced a rapidly changing environment that threatened its existence as new competitive offerings overtook its core products. But it enjoyed solid relationships with a client roster of blue-chip companies across a range of industries. It had a war chest equal to 50 percent of its annual revenues that could be applied to new initiatives and acquisitions, and it had secured the approval of its parent company to move forward with a growth strategy. Company leaders saw an opportunity to create a new market offering that blended existing products with innovative solutions capabilities.

Seven Crucial Steps

Here are their stories and the seven crucial steps that made the difference between success and failure:

1. Find Your Intrinsic Competitive Advantage

As we have said repeatedly, every company must uncover its competitive advantage. Both companies developed positioning statements. Company A fine-tuned its strategy by building on the company's successful past and offering a clearer and more compelling explanation of the benefits it provided its stakeholders. Company B went further, redefining itself so as to build on its successful manufacturing track record. They sought to create a new category with comprehensive solutions that addressed key needs championed within customer and industry circles. Each company found an opportunity to identify hidden value, and each articulated that value in a way that differentiated it from the competition. So far, so good.

2. Begin with the End in Mind

Stephen Covey's principle means to pursue actions based on a clearly identified outcome, which, of course, makes it harder to do. Over a period of months, the leaders of both companies brought key groups of decision makers together to analyze their competitive environments, assess their own capabilities, and ask and answer the tough questions. *What is the desired outcome we want to achieve? What do we hope to accomplish by pursuing this strategy? How will executing this tactic help support our plan?* "End in mind" questions help keep you focused and on track. Each company's leaders emerged from the strategic planning process with a set of clearly identified objectives and a well-thought-out im-

plementation plan. Executives at both companies were ener-
gized, optimistic, and enthusiastic.

3. Align Interests

Both companies began implementing their plans. Yet market conditions began to exert negative pressure, resulting in regulatory
changes, increasing investor demands, and elusive targets for sales
and profits. In response, executives at Company A remained committed to their objective and aligned in their actions. Executives at
Company B did not. Company A pursued a growth strategy
relentlessly even when their stock price dropped by half. Company B began to vacillate on plans and commitments and soon
implemented cost-cutting tactics that were equally relentless—
even as these same executives talked about the need to grow bigger, faster. Alignment and consistency matter, especially in times
of change and uncertainty. The lack of alignment and lack of commitment to the plan was the beginning of the end for Company B.
Continued alignment at Company A meant the start of something
new and increasingly valuable.

4. Think Strategically, Not Tactically

Leaders at Company A implemented broad strategic initiatives in
key divisions and launched a program to ensure that all constituencies understood where the company was going and why.
Rather than playing its winning hand, Company B resorted to
cost-cutting in the face of industry downturns—even though key
market segments the company had targeted for sales were
largely unaffected. It began to play not to lose: scrutinizing costs
again and again; freezing all spending and investment; cutting
staff to the bone. These were tactics, not strategies. Paralysis
ensued. If you ever fall into this trap, you must pull yourself out
by focusing on strategies that leverage your competitive advantage. Remember: tactics without strategy is stupidity.

5. Do Something Meaningful, Yet Achievable

Company A did not try to change its world overnight. It began
with small steps, and built on those. These steps ranged from a

web site overhaul to creating new divisions and branding initiatives—all company firsts, all done methodically, step-by-step, with a common strategy in mind. Meanwhile, Company B spent time and money on nonessential items, such as a logo redesign. It failed to pursue qualified sales leads captured at industry trade shows. Its engineering department missed deadline after deadline on product enhancements and new product launches. Celebrating victories requires having some victories to celebrate.

6. Get a Checkup from the Neck Up

As a leader, are you saying and doing the things that your people need to hear and see to believe in what the company is doing, and to give their best efforts to help you get there? You reflect your attitude in your speech, your body language, your actions. Do you manipulate your people like chessboard pawns or treat them as people with cares, concerns, and needs just like yours? Guess which attitude builds a company and which one stops a company in its tracks. Company A continued to articulate a compelling marketplace value proposition and deliver on its promises. By contrast the top executives at Company B often disagreed with one another and failed to reach consensus on even the simplest action items. The top two executives withdrew from sight and confined themselves to their own offices. The signal sent by these smart but otherwise unwitting executives was all too clear inside and outside the company. Pessimism, staff departures, and more missed sales and deadlines followed.

7. Be Accountable

Business leaders must hold themselves accountable for implementing the strategies they originally agreed to pursue—and they sometimes need help from outsiders, almost acting as their conscience. Nothing happens just because we say it or write it down. True change must start at the top before it can be embraced throughout a company. Over a four-year period, Company A exploded in size as its annual revenue quadrupled and its profit margins climbed. Two years later, Company B watched their critical engineering developments fall further behind the competitive curve as peer companies continued to improve, refine, and market alternative solutions. Company B is a shadow of its former self, its war chest has been depleted, and most of the senior management team has departed. It has been reduced to watching from the sidelines as its industry begins the early stages of recovery

● ● ●

These seven steps are not difficult to understand and appreciate. Yet it is amazing to think about how uncommon common sense really is. In these two cases, the ability (or inability) to implement these seven deceptively simple steps when confronting change and uncertainty has made all the difference.

Part 5

Leveraging Change in Good Times

"All I'm saying is <u>now</u> is the time to develop the technology to deflect an asteroid."

19

If It's Not Broken, Break It, Then Fix It

W hat waves of change crashing toward your organization will make your currently profitable business plan obsolete? Sound like an improbable scenario? It doesn't seem improbable to:

- Successful advertisers and their agencies, who are scrambling to find new ways to reach and engage consumers in an increasingly cluttered and fragmented media market made even tougher by technology that allows people to delete or bypass commercials
- Pharmaceutical company leaders who must constantly develop and bring to market new high-quality medical products to replace revenue lost to expiring patents and generic drug-makers
- Recording industry executives who, in a span of twenty years, have watched the way music is sold and enjoyed move from vinyl LPs to CDs to music that's now available (sometimes for free) over the Internet
- Packaged-goods manufacturers who have watched store brands capture an increasingly larger share of sales since the early 1990s

Some threats, though difficult to spot, can be relatively easy to quantify and address. Other hard-to-spot dangers are even harder to assess in terms of the potential negative impact on your organization. You might easily recognize still other threats but dismiss them as harmless.

Tom Leppert, chief executive of the $6.5 billion Turner Construction Co. lived in Hawaii for ten years. He observes that the five companies that dominated Hawaii's economy twenty-five years ago no longer exist. Similar changes have buffeted the Fortune 500 companies over the same time period.[88]

For years, through boom times and downturns, companies winning the Dallas 100 award have achieved an average annual compound growth rate of 150 percent, some generating up to $200 million a year in sales. Yet each year, many of these high-flying companies succumb to the double whammy of fast growth and a higher profile that invites new pressure from their competition. Over a thirteen-year period, out of literally thousands of companies nominated for the award, only seventy-one companies have been recognized for three years of record-setting growth, and only one company has won the award for stellar growth eight times in a thirteen-year period.[89]

The lesson is clear. Whether you're running a large company or small business, you must be ready with the next generation of thinking and remain alert to changes, especially those outside your control, even when your business is meeting your operational expectations and hitting your financial objectives. If you fail to respond to changing market conditions, you could find yourself "making buggy whips" and entering a death spiral.

A Successful Past Doesn't Guarantee a Successful Future

According to *Family Business*, most companies of all types and sizes fail within twenty years of their founding. Among family companies, "less than 30 percent survive into the second generation, barely 10 percent make it to the third, and only about 4 percent to the fourth."[90]

America's oldest company is Zildjian Cymbal Co., founded in 1623 in Constantinople and now based in Norwell, Massachusetts. The oldest company founded in the US is Tuttle Farm, which John Tuttle founded around 1635 after leaving England

and surviving a shipwreck off the coast of Maine. Mighty Cargill of Minnesota, the world's largest private company with annual revenue of $50 billion, was formed in 1865.[91]

Some companies have thrived because they decided to remain small. About half of the 102 companies on the list of "America's oldest family companies" compiled by *Family Business* employ fewer than fifteen people. Many have fewer than ten. All but three companies on this list are private, having avoided the temptations of a public stock offering.[92]

From other companies that have started small and grown big—companies like Corning (1851), Levi Strauss & Co. and King Ranch (both 1853), Anheuser-Busch Cos. (1860), Bacardi (1862), R.R. Donnelly & Sons (1864), Miliken & Co (1865), and J.C. Penney (1902)—one can learn important secrets.

What's the secret to the longevity of these venerable old companies? What lessons can we learn from them? How do successful companies maintain their performance in times of change and uncertainty? Why do otherwise successful companies stumble? What can be done to prevent it? Eric Hoffer, author and Presidential Medal of Freedom winner, suggested in 1932, "In a time of drastic change, it is the learners who inherit the future. The learned usually find themselves equipped to live in a world that no longer exists."[93]

Yet learning and changing come hard to many. Making changes goes against human nature, especially when business appears to be going well. Most of us are content to stay rooted in the familiar. Stability and constancy are great qualities, but in times of "drastic change" such strengths can become weaknesses.

To simplify, there are two kinds of leaders where change is concerned:

- Those who think about the future and determine how best to position their organizations to capitalize on emerging trends
- Those who choose to respond to changes that threaten their organizations

"Drive thy business or it will drive thee," said Benjamin Franklin. Hundreds of years later, Jack Welch, legendary former chief executive of GE, echoed Franklin's advice when he said, "Control your destiny or someone else will."[94]

The Four Cs

Leaders of successful organizations who are willing to make significant changes, even when things are going well, bring a balance of vision and pragmatism that we summarize as "The Four Cs":

- Commitment to Excellence
- Continuous Learning
- Conservatism in Financing
- Courageous Decision Making.

1. Commitment to Excellence

To become and remain successful, you must accept only the best: the smartest talent, the highest standards, the greatest work, the best results. Remaining committed to excellence means resisting the tendency to cut corners, skip steps, and settle for average performance in certain areas when other parts of the company are doing well. Dan Scoggin, who took T.G.I. Friday's from a singles bar in New York to a worldwide chain, called this comfortable mode the "success syndrome." It's up to you to articulate the meaning of excellence throughout the organization's values, mission, objectives, and direction. Your ability to do so will infuse excellence in your team's performance. The best companies set the bar high and then continue to raise it. So you must critique your organization on a continuous basis.

Often sustaining excellence requires that you have the courage to "break it and then fix it," because the chances are good that what worked before won't work today, much less tomorrow. J.C. Penney, for instance, was founded in 1902 with a commitment to customer service. That focus is very much alive today. But though their operation was strong, they broke, then fixed it. They modified it to reflect changes in the retail industry such as offshore manufacturing, centralized buying, and shifting consumer habits. "I cannot emphasize enough the importance of remembering your core values," says chief executive Allen Questrom. "We increased our advertising budget $100 million in a very difficult time to communicate that J.C. Penney is all about fashion [because] we determined that our customers want Neiman-Marcus fashion at J.C. Penney prices. Today, we make every cent count for our customers. And we set new standards for excellence in our people."[95]

Whatever your goal, make certain it's clear to everyone. Meanwhile, your company's commitment to high standards and continuous improvement must never waver. Successful companies know that good enough never is.

2. Continuous Learning

Great leaders emphasize the importance of continuous learning as an enterprise-wide responsibility, not one confined to the R&D department. It's an acquired state of being that encourages and rewards all employees to remain observant, inquisitive, and imaginative. Continuous learning scatters the seeds of money-making and money-saving ideas throughout all levels of your organization. The trick is giving these seeds an environment where they can take root and blossom. If leaders do not embed innovation (the by-product of continuous learning) in an organization's culture, the organization will ignore or underfund it when tough times threaten the bottom line.

A company committed to continuous learning will set employees free to explore, test, and even fail at new ventures. Learning continuously means making mistakes, which takes courage, especially in the face of quarterly earnings reports.

Some organizations make innovation every person's responsibility. Others create teams that assemble and then disperse once they have addressed a particular problem or opportunity. Still others assign a senior-level person to drive innovation. At Amazon, Chief Executive Jeff Bezos brings in guest speakers from all walks of life on a regular basis to posit scenarios that get his troops' juices flowing. An MIT physicist, for example, asked Amazon employees to imagine the day customers could custom-design, build, order, and buy through Amazon any product they desired.[96]

You must find and implement the approach to continuous learning that works for you and your organization. You must question premises, challenge conventions, and ask "*What if?*" to keep smart people sharp and eager to learn. Call it calisthenics for the mind. In addition, you must provide the tools, resources, people, and encouragement necessary to jump-start and institutionalize the creative process. Such an environment keeps people on their toes, heightens the excitement and purpose within an organization, and can lead to your next product, service, or operational breakthrough. We will explore innovation in more depth in chapter 22.

3. Conservative Financial Management

As we've already observed, cash is king, and successful companies make it, save it, and use it wisely. Don't confuse, however, a conservative approach to fiscal management with an aversion to risk. And don't let a fun-loving image mask what in reality is an approach that's thoughtful, disciplined, and effective.

Southwest Airlines, a company with a fun, easy-going and occasionally wacky persona, takes financial management seriously. Chief Executive Gary Kelly and President Colleen Barrett use Southwest's war chests strategically, prudently, and effectively. Kelly and Barrett intend to grow the airline 8 percent annually as they look for ways to increase the company's 10 percent share of domestic airline traffic.[97] So while some airline carriers have eliminated 10 to 15 percent of seat capacity, Southwest has expanded and grown as much as their rivals have cut. After American Airlines reduced its service from its St. Louis hub, for example, Southwest moved quickly to add new flights.[98] All this stems from its conservative approach to financial management.

Even when business is going well, smart leaders should reexamine their approach to business. This may involve weeding out unprofitable customers. CRI, a marketing-research company that had stopped growing, found that their relationships with big, well-known companies were actually less profitable than with their smaller ones. CRI's leaders made the difficult decision to turn away business from clients that had helped build the firm. Over ten years, CRI reduced its roster of clients while increasing its revenue from $11 to $30 million.[99] Smart executives understand how their companies make their money, what it costs to serve customers, and when to make a break from the past in order to maintain their edge in changing times.

4. Courageous Decision Making

High standards, an environment that nurtures innovation, and prudent financial management provide the foundation of successful companies. If the future of the company is on the line, company leaders can choose to stay the course and try to ride out the threat. Or they can make proactive, courageous decisions.

Courageous decisions define people and organizations. Intel in the mid-1980s faced an assault on the memory chip business that Intel had perfected. Japanese competitors had mastered the production process and now offered chips at much lower prices than those of Intel's. Andy Grove tells how he and cofounder Gordon Moore studied and debated options ranging from building new plants to developing new versions of chips with special-purpose memories. These options, however, did not appear to counter the growing threat; company leadership was "wandering in the valley of death." Finally in 1985, Grove and Moore made a courageous decision: abandon the memory chip business and focus on microprocessors, even though this meant abandoning Intel's corporate identity. Grove asked Moore the mother of all "What if?" questions: "If we got kicked out and the board brought in a new chief executive, what do you think he would do?" Gordon answered without hesitation, "He would get us out of memories."[100] That's exactly what Grove and Moore did. Grove and Moore made a courageous decision that caused the company to break with a plan that had worked and fix its future on a market that ultimately has made the company even more valuable.

Sometimes there is a fifth "C." Less universal than the previous four, this one pertains particularly to leaders who are trying to take their companies to higher levels of success.

5. Creating Crises to Increase Focus and Urgency

Some companies excel more at responding to threats than to opportunities. So creating a crisis—"breaking it"—can provide a wake-up call for organizations that have grown rich, happy, and complacent. Of course, a leader who values his or her credibility would never create a phony crisis. Instead, in order to demonstrate that survival demands imminent, radical change, the leader forces the company to zero in on a particular area of business that faces an emerging threat. Such a threat usually falls into one of three categories: financial (including hostile takeovers), customer-related, or industry driven (including regulatory matters).

In 1990, Craig Weatherup, the head of Pepsi-Cola's profitable $7 billion soft drink division, feared that a business-as-usual approach in his highly competitive industry would not secure the company's future success. So he created a financial crisis. He ordered his managers to increase their customary 10 percent profit target to 15 percent. Sharing negative feedback from some of Pepsi's most important customers, Weatherup gave each of his lieutenants ninety days to determine ways the company could better serve customers while increasing profitability. The lieutenants used the data and knowledge they gathered to train the next layer of management, which in turn replicated the process until it ultimately reached some thirty thousand employees. As a result of this created crisis, Pepsi-Cola reorganized itself into 107 units that focus on producing results at the customer level. Three years later, profits for the first quarter of 1993 rose 22 percent.[101]

Our firm's experience indicates that, more times than not, a leader faces the choice of continued success versus gradual decline. All too often, today's leaders disregard warning signs, choose to look the other way, or genuinely believe that their organizations are safe from the waves of change.

Arthur Andersen & Co. was doing quite well with its blue-chip roster of clients when it self-immolated in the Enron scandal. Whether you take the sympathetic view that management didn't know what was happening or the more skeptical position that the firm's culture encouraged bad behavior, the result was the same. A company founded in 1913 and built on trust was toppled in a matter of weeks by the misdeeds of a few misguided partners. Andersen's collapse provides a twenty-first century reminder to leaders of even the most successful organizations that they must watch for, root out, and quash such behavior, lest it creep in and undermine the organization's future.

Winston Churchill said that, "To improve is to change; to be perfect is to change often." In *The Road Ahead*, Bill Gates reminds us that, "Success is a lousy teacher. It seduces smart people into thinking they can't lose. And it's an unreliable guide to the future."

So even if your business isn't broken, you might want to think seriously about breaking it and then fixing it—before you're forced to do so.

"Somewhere out there, Patrick, is the key to increased sales. I want you to find that key, Patrick, and bring it to me."

20

There's Always Room for Growth

Most leaders say they want to grow their organizations. Let's be clear from the start. Not all growth is good. Growth—particularly fast growth—can be expensive to fund, disruptive to cultures, upsetting to customers, and occasionally disastrous to organizations that aren't ready for it. Consequently, leaders of many organizations make a point of staying small. They avoid the headaches of running a large operation, appeal to a select constituent base, and remain satisfied with a relatively stable financial result. These enterprises can range from boutique professional firms offering highly specialized services for small industry segments, to specialty retail shops, to elite schools that accept only certain types of students. The specialized focus, combined with a reputation for delivering quality products or services, may allow these organizations to charge premium prices.

Yet for most companies, the need for growth is genuine and acute. Growth for them, in other words, is good. The risk of not growing exceeds any risk associated with growing, because leaders that choose not to grow eventually cede market share and profits to the competition. They may be ceding the future as well.

For those leaders that want to grow but find their organizations at a plateau, what's to be done? After all, even in good times, don't leaders of successful enterprises find themselves toiling in industries that appear saturated, with little or no room for growth? Is it foolish to believe that growth opportunities exist in mature industries? Is the only way to grow by expanding geographically?

No. That line of questioning dooms a company to mediocrity and, perhaps, failure. Leaders who embrace uncertainty, question premises, and turn obstacles into opportunities become tomorrow's winners. Such leaders commit to making whatever substantive changes are required. They tend to challenge conventional wisdom and the status-quo.

Larry Bossidy is one such leader. "There's no such thing as a mature market," he declares. As chief executive of AlliedSignal, Bossidy sought "mature executives who can find ways to grow."[102] Bossidy served notice to his team in the early 1990s not to consider any market as fully penetrated, citing such businesses as Home Depot and Circuit City, which entered already penetrated markets and dominated them.[103] Bossidy identified and then fixed many of the growth problems he encountered at AlliedSignal. His lieutenants found new ways to help the company grow. The growth initiatives that Bossidy and his team embarked on and implemented throughout the 1990s quintupled the market value of AlliedSignal shares and significantly outperformed the Dow Jones Industrial Average and the S&P 500, setting the stage for AlliedSignal's merger with Honeywell in December, 1999.[104]

"The only company that continues to enjoy success," said the late Roberto Goizueta, chief executive of Coca-Cola, "is the company that keeps struggling to achieve it."[105]

But how? What steps can large organizations that already enjoy significant market share take to move to the next level of success? We'll examine ways to institutionalize change throughout the organization in subsequent chapters, but for now we'll examine the ingredients you must combine to develop a successful growth recipe.

Four Approaches to Profitable Growth

These ingredients for growth involve shifts in position and perspective. You must shift your position so as to view things from the perspective of what customers want rather than what your company is trying to sell to them. Those are often two entirely different expectation sets. When you start outside your organization by listening to and observing customers, opportunities will emerge. Here are four distinct approaches for creating sustainable, profitable growth.

1. Change Your Category

When Roberto Goizueta became president of Coca-Cola in 1980, the soft-drink business was, as it still is today, fiercely competitive. Coca-Cola claimed about one-third of what was considered a mature US soft-drink market. But Goizueta did not believe the market was mature. What, he asked his executives, was the average per-capita daily consumption of fluids by the world's 4.4 billion people? His executives said it was sixty-four ounces. What, Goizueta then asked, is the daily per-capita consumption of Coca-Cola? Less than two ounces, he was told. Finally, Goizueta wanted to know Coca-Cola's worldwide "market share of the stomach." The company's impact here was negligible. In the hard-fought cola wars, Coca-Cola had viewed Pepsi as the enemy. Goizueta helped the company's leaders reframe the battle for the "share of the stomach" in terms of water, coffee, juice, milk and tea. With a series of fundamentally simple questions to his key executives, Goizueta changed the game for Coca-Cola by effectively changing the category.[106]

In the case of Coca-Cola, Goizueta shifted his perspective so that it was focused outside the company looking in versus inside looking out. This shift helped Goizueta see new ways of meeting his customers' total needs, and it at once illustrates through a spectacular success a principle articulated by Ram

Charan and Noel Tichy in *Every Business Is a Growth Business*:
the power of a strategy built around giving customers more of
what they already want.[107]

2. Address Your Customers' Total Needs

Kinko's opened its first store in 1970 as a copier center. Its
expanded hours providing copying and binding services on a
round-the-clock basis effectively tapped into the "faster-better-
cheaper" mentality of the information age and Internet boom.
Kinko's continued to expand its service offerings, and as a result
has derived an increasing percentage of its revenue by providing computer and Internet access and other administrative services for what the company calls the "mobile professional."[108]
Today, the company operates more than twelve hundred cen-
ters, and chief executive Gary Kuzin says the "image of Kinko's
as your corner copy shop [has] been fading for five years. We
really serve as the back office for our business customers."[109]
Kinko's has grown (and recently been acquired by FedEx for
$2.4 billion) because it has kept finding new ways to serve its
customers' total needs.

3. Find or Create New Segments That Are Growing

A third route to growth is finding new segments to serve. For Nextel
Communications, this route has proven to be a winning strategy.

Nextel was a late entrant to the telecommunications market
already crowded with well-established cellular phone providers
such as Ericsson, Nokia, and Fujitsu. Sales and marketing efforts
focused on the growing consumer base of cell phone users.
Advertising messages appealed to consumers with messages and
images that were largely price and feature driven. Sales grew
nicely but leveled off after several months. More players were
joining the cell-phone party, and they were also using price and

feature messages in their sales and marketing efforts. The problem became a familiar one. How could Nextel continue to grow?

Nextel held the winning idea in its hands. The company's distinctive phone design included a two-way walkie-talkie capability, in a package five times smaller than a walkie-talkie, that allowed subscribers to connect directly with other callers for a fraction of regular cellular calling costs. Because of the phone's direct- connect capability, workforces could use the walkie-talkie features of the phone and stay connected directly without having to dial through a more expensive cellular network. By shifting the promotional focus to workforce cell-phone users and communicating the benefits of efficiency (faster, easier connections) versus price, Nextel created a new category for business communications, thereby leveraging its competitive advantage and attaining new sales growth. While Nextel has continued to broaden the scope of its sales and marketing efforts, the company has remained steadfast in communicating the unique benefits of its phone and network to a distinct audience of business users. Therein lies its present-day success.

4. Capitalize on New Opportunities

This approach requires insight, courage, and patience.

The University of Texas at Austin's College of Communication is among the nation's best schools for students wishing to pursue careers in advertising, public relations, journalism, advertising, radio, TV, and film. For years the college has attracted the best students while building a reputation for producing engaging documentary and experimental films. At the same time, the city of Austin has become regarded as a great place to produce commercially successful films, as demonstrated by *Spy Kids III*, *Once Upon a Time in Mexico*, *Second Hand Lions*, *School of Rock*, and *The Alamo*. Austin also is home to technology companies that are forging the marriage of technology and entertainment in the development of digital cinema. Still, UT could not move out from the shadows cast by USC, UCLA, and NYU. What could the school do to enter the same league as its rivals?

"We spoke frankly with our alumni and friends in the entertainment industry," says Ellen Wartella, the college's dean. "We asked them what we could do to better prepare students for the commercial film industry. They said, 'Make [the experience] real.'"[110] To enhance students' film-making experience, UT created a public-private partnership, forming the UT Film Institute and an affiliated production company, Burnt Orange Productions. Together, they will train students to develop specialized skills in producing, directing, cinematography, editing, sound design, and production design. Students will apprentice with faculty and top professionals drawn from Hollywood and Texas on films produced through Burnt Orange Productions. UT chose Advanced Micro Devices as its technology partner so that students can be trained in digital production, the new Hollywood standard. Moreover, it hired a veteran film executive to run its for-profit venture. It assembled a blue-chip roster of twenty-four advisors, including actor Matthew McConaughey, Motion Picture Association of America president Jack Valenti, Sony Pictures Classics copresident Michael Barker, and WB Co-Chief Executive Jordan Levin. The school has also signed investors to help fund the venture. Johnnie Ray, UT's vice president for development, observes, "The growing commercial power of independent films along with the emergence of digital filmmaking revolution in Texas puts UT Austin in the driver's seat."[111]

Time will tell if this venture is successful. But to listen to the experts, this move by UT to build a new core competency around one where it enjoyed a proven track record of achievement is a formula for success. UT's bold initiative "will revolutionize the face of film education and the way filmmakers are trained in this country," says Thom Mount, head of production for RKO Pictures.[112]

Before you consider your market saturated, try thinking about it in a new way. A shift in perspective may result in a positive shift in your organization's profitable growth.

"You have to admit that your chip looks a lot like their chip."

21

The Longbow
Make Innovation Your Secret Weapon

Tastes evolve. Habits change. New expectations develop. For leaders that can read these shifting behavioral sands and then effectively develop and introduce products or services that address them, such changes represent new opportunities for their companies to widen the gap between themselves and their competitors.

It's no wonder, then, that product innovation forms the essence of many winning organizations' competitive advantage. Effective new product development and implementation can help companies maintain customer loyalty, penetrate new markets, expand market share, and generate increased profits.

The desire to expand territory and fill the corporate coffers is as old as human nature. And relying on innovation as the source of an organization's competitive advantage is a time-tested strategy.

Consider how technological advancement has continually transformed warfare. In 1346, England's Edward III had invaded France, sacking Caen before retreating to Crecy near the coast. France's Philip VI pursued Edward, caught up with his forces and readied his attack. Edward's army of between twelve and twenty thousand knights and archers prepared to meet a force of at least forty thousand French cavalry sheathed in armor and six thousand Genoese mercenaries armed with crossbows. What the English lacked in numbers they countered with superb organization and superior weaponry.

175

Until the Battle of Crecy, knights had fought one another on horseback. Now a new weapon—unleashed as never before on this day—would change the way future wars were waged. Edward arrayed his troops in an open V toward the French in a two-thousand-yard battle line, instructing his knights to dismount and his archers to move forward. Philip counseled patience, but his generals, hot with emotion, refused to delay the attack. Philip's troops began to advance without any apparent order.

Edward's competitive advantage was the longbow. This weapon enabled highly trained archers to fire more arrows than crossbows (ten to twenty per minute) and fire them farther (up to 250 yards) with armor-piercing force. As the first wave of Genoese cross-bowmen advanced, Edward signaled his archers, who rained more than thirty thousand arrows down on the Genoese such "that it seemed as if it snowed."[113] Thousands of the Genoese crossbowmen and then thousands more French knights and their squires were killed in the first few minutes of battle, disrupting what order existed and devastating morale. At the conclusion of the eight-hour battle, the French had lost up to ten thousand men while the English lost just several hundred. The victory at Crecy went to Edward, and the longbow changed the way battles were fought for the next fifty years as England relied on its revolutionary weapon to dominate its rivals.

We've often recounted this fourteenth-century story as a lesson to present-day leaders, coining the phrase "longbow marketing" to describe a strategy by which savvy marketers can achieve a competitive advantage over their rivals in the ongoing battle for customers. There are four principal ways to apply a longbow strategy to the product development process, and we'll examine each in turn. First, however, I want to emphasize the importance of preparing yourself to commit to innovation.

Prepare Your Mind

Most new products fail. Increased competition, market fragmentation, shorter product life cycles, time-to-market issues, and increased costs are the enemies of a new product's success. Sadly, a more dangerous enemy of innovation is the mindset of a leader that fails to make new product development a critical component of the organization's culture.

How important is innovation? A study released in 2003 by Drs. Robert G. Cooper and Scott J. Edgett of the Product Development Institute found that "leaders in product innovation derive 43% of their profits from new products, while average companies achieve only 28%." And this same study found that "average performers in product innovation did not meet their sales, profit and market-share objectives 50% of the time."[114] In other words, organizations that commit themselves to innovation are more likely to experience greater success than peer organizations that do not.

In a series of surveys our firm conducted in 2002 at the height of a recession, we asked business leaders, "Which areas of executive performance were most rewarded?" In other words, what are your priorities for working your way out of the recession? Out of six business drivers we listed—technical knowledge, innovation, operational efficiency, identifying and implementing initiatives to create new revenue, employee retention/development of talent, and building and maintaining relationships with partners, regulators, and/or investors—innovation ranked dead last among businesses with less than $50 million in annual revenue. Among companies with $50 million or more in annual revenue, innovation ranked first. These findings indicate that the smaller the company, the less likely its top executives are committed to funding innovation, at least in uncertain times. As we'll discuss in chapter 25, cutting R&D budgets in difficult times is mortgaging the future. Conventional wisdom suggests that in good times and tough times smaller companies should scramble for every advantage they can get. So it would seem logical that they would look for and expect to find that advantage—as Edward's outnumbered army found it—in the form of an effective new weapon. Unfortunately, management's impatience or lack of conviction can dampen new product development in even the best of times. It's imperative that you commit yourself and your organization to innovation.

I've included at the end of this chapter a highly simplified new-product-development diagram showing the six key phases of new product design and development. I have reduced further these six phases into four areas in order to show how observation, insights, and the lessons of King Edward's longbow strategy can help you to revitalize your approach to innovation and emerge victorious in the battle for market share.

1. Idea Generation

Good products come from good ideas. Turning ideas into products is both an art and a science, and successful companies master the product-development process and elevate it to higher levels of effectiveness year after year. But where exactly do good ideas come from? Mostly by watching, asking, and listening to your customers and competitors. A thorough analysis of the product category, competitive insights, and consumer issues can help you understand market trends and other factors. As we discussed in chapter 12, there's plenty of data out there. The key is understanding which data is most important, knowing where to find it, and then, having secured it, interpreting it correctly to determine needs, gaps, or deficiencies in the marketplace.

Armed with this data and the insights the data suggest, conduct brainstorm sessions involving your major departments to hatch possible ideas for addressing the opportunities. Then screen these ideas to pare the list to those that seem to have the most potential. Exploratory research may help further qualify promising ideas.

But be careful about tossing out a concept or objective that may at first seem impractical, unmanageable, or unattainable. Post-it Notes and Viagra both failed initial tests. So don't punish failures or throw in the towel if an idea doesn't work the first time. Failure is part of a process that can lead to success.

Conversely, ideas that look like sure-fire winners can fade over time. Starting in April 1860, the Pony Express operated as the fastest mail delivery system between St. Joseph, Missouri, and Sacramento, California. Customers were willing to pay rates that were well above standard mail delivery in return for speedy service. But the completion of the telegraph line eighteen months later rendered the service obsolete. Yet this success-turned-failure offers a valuable history lesson. About one hundred years later, Fred Smith became convinced that customers would pay much higher delivery rates for overnight service, and he transformed FedEx into a modern-day version of the Pony Express.[115] Fred Smith's good idea became his longbow.

A longbow redefines the category. Consequently, a longbow is not a survival gambit, but rather a means for mounting an offensive and changing the way the battle for customers is fought. FedEx delivered mail and packages that "absolutely, positively" had to be in the recipients' hands the next day. Dell eliminated a step in the sales process by enabling customers to order PCs directly from the manufacturer. Wal-Mart brought volume discounts to small-town shoppers. American Airlines rewarded its best customers with a first-of-its-kind frequent flier program. In each case, the winning company introduced a new idea—simpler approach, better value, greater convenience—that shifted the battle lines and gave those holding a longbow a distinct competitive advantage. Another characteristic that separates a longbow idea from any other new product (especially a line extension of an existing product) is that it cannot be readily countered or duplicated by competitors. Where the Pony Express was countered by the telegraph, FedEx has used its longbow over the years to maintain and grow its market share despite thrusts from the U.S. Postal Service and UPS. There's no substitute for watching, listening to, and learning from your customers. Many times, they will help spark your next big idea.

2. Product Design and Development

Not all new products, of course, are longbows. Whether you're designing and developing a longbow or refining, updating, or enhancing an existing product, your process must be fast, efficient, and produce a product that your customers really want. Kurt Swogger, vice president at Dow Chemical Company's Polyolefins and Elastomers R&D unit, says speedy product development helps Dow "make more money."[116] Dow's performance in reducing the company's time to market has made them the gold standard in the product development world.[117]

Importantly, speed does not sacrifice safety, thoroughness, or quality. It's an attitude that permeates the organization, accelerating the design and development phase. Because time to market is such a critical factor in determining a new product's success, leaders must always look for ways to improve efficiency. Mike Wilkinson, chief executive of Paragon Innovations, an engineering firm that helps companies like 3M, Baxter, and Hitachi with their design and development issues, stresses the importance of building efficiency into the development process at the outset in order to circumvent time delays, cost overruns, and manufacturing problems. Such planning enables smart companies to bridge the usual gap between the design and manufacturing phases so that products can be manufactured reliably. A system that provides a step-by-step approach for product enhancements, recalibrations, and modifications is essential in order to ensure the effective, efficient manufacturing of a high-quality product.

PepsiCo's Frito-Lay division, for example, has been extremely efficient in developing and introducing new products that build on the success of existing products, such as new flavors (guacamole-flavored Doritos), new shapes (Twisted Cheetos), and new offerings that compete with a competitor's existing product (Lay's Stax versus Procter & Gamble's Pringles). [118] Additionally, Frito-Lay and other food makers like Kraft and fast food restaurants like McDonald's, Wendy's, and Burger King are responding to the nation's obesity problem by tweaking existing products and introducing new ones. "We're not going to do anything radical," said a Kraft spokesperson. "This is about making small, incremental changes."[119]

There's no question that "small, incremental changes" can add up to big dollars. They can help a company maintain or even grow market share, but they rarely change the landscape of the battle. Longbow development, by contrast, is not focused on incremental change, but rather on radical change that will drive double-digit revenue growth. The longbow's beauty and power lie in its simplicity. A longbow leverages a company's existing quality, idea, or characteristic that can become a strategic advantage because competitors don't have it. Because of its low production costs, for instance, Toyota was able to develop the Lexus and redefine value in the luxury automobile segment.

By leveraging the competitive advantage that I believe exists within every company, a longbow is more difficult for competitors to duplicate. Home Depot redefined retailing when it married the do-it-yourself hardware store with the concept of the superstore warehouse. While others have joined this retailing segment or tried to shift their model to capture a slice of this market, Home Depot's competitors can't keep pace without expanding their existing outlets or building new ones. These examples illustrate that customers wanted the concepts, products or services these companies developed, and a speedy and efficient design and development process enabled the company to achieve competitive advantage—to transform the opportunity into a longbow.

3. Pricing, Channel Business Model Development

Between the time your company tests a product prototype and brings the final product to market, you must make a series of determinations about distribution channels, business model, and product price. Simply inventing a better mousetrap is no guarantee that your product will find its way into the hands of customers, much less that a purchase of your product will yield a profit. The chief executive of a small company we have advised has developed a new lighting device utilizing LED technology. Third-party laboratory testing of this lighting product against industry giants such as GE, Philips, and Sylvania has shown the new product to out-perform its rivals. But these competitors have shown they will disrupt the flow of raw materials the smaller company needs, threatening production. And many of these competitors are flexing their financial muscle with distributors and customers to dissuade them from buying the new product. Though it's too soon to say, early indications are that without securing a partner that can leverage its own reputation, financial wherewithal, and distribution network, this start-up will continue to struggle and may ultimately be doomed to failure—despite having a superb product. Conversely, if a company can secure a partner looking to fill gaps in its own product portfolio, together they can help turn the tables on the competition. Smaller companies trying to gain a foothold—and even larger companies that are attempting to enter new market segments with innovative products or services—must realize that today's environment makes the go-it-alone approach riskier than ever.

Size, speed, experience, and reputation are all weapons that must be deployed in the new product battle. Gillette is using its huge distribution network to increase sales of disposable razors and "shaving systems" in Europe and Latin America, much to Wall Street's delight.[120]

Pricing, likewise, is a science that will determine whether a product succeeds or fails. Commodity producers often employ a low-product-cost strategy, while a low-development-cost strategy focuses on developing products on a tight budget. The pricing phase involves anticipating the competition's response, establishing the profit margin, and then setting a price that customers are willing to pay. For a longbow to produce the best results, you must solve the pricing riddle and operate other aspects of your business effectively. That's because a longbow will focus attention on your category, raise customer expectations, and punish you if you fail to meet them or set the wrong price.

4. Product Launch and Ongoing Support Process

Your idea has become a prototype; you've determined distribution channels and set a price. You must take one more step before you send your product into full-scale battle: test marketing. This step allows you to correct little mistakes and to gauge, on a larger scale than a prototype allows but a smaller scale than a market-wide launch, the product's performance, production efficiency, inventory control, and marketing effectiveness. You must weigh the rewards of learning this information against the risks of tele-graphing your plans to the enemy, the competition. Some leaders also use the test market process to condition the market, including employees and suppliers, prior to the actual introduction. By the time you're ready to proceed with your main launch, you must give it everything you've got. Just as Edward's troops loosed "arrows [that] fell like snow," so, too, must your troops give your new product introduction everything they've got. Given the high death rate of new products, a half-hearted effort will be fatal.

Launching a longbow attack provides another advantage: your customers easily recognize its value. The "Intel Inside" campaign has taken Intel out from inside the computer and shifted the battle from the invisible chips once considered com-modities to a premium-priced market for its super-small, super-efficient chips—where its "time-pacing" approach to product innovation gives the company a clear superiority. (Intel pushes itself to adhere to the pace of Moore's law, named for cofounder Gordon E. Moore, who predicted the number of transistors that can be designed into a given space should double every eighteen months.) During and after the launch, any new product demands that a company provide ongoing support to dealers and distribu-tors, suppliers and partners, employees and customers.

A longbow will change the way your organization works. More than thirty years ago, Southwest Airlines reshaped the air-line industry with a low-price, customer-centered philosophy. Today as then, its employees are measured on attitude first and aptitude second, sustaining a reputation (and stock price) that was launched with a revolutionary approach to a mature business.

Business is a high-stakes war in which companies fiercely battle for customers. Take a page from history and then take a fresh look at how your company approaches product development. You may discover a secret weapon that will repel your competition while helping you win new customers and grow your profits.

Product development

BUSTIN & CO.

Phase 1 Discovery	Phase 2 Validation	Phase 3 Design	Phase 4 Development	Phase 5 Test	Phase 6 Launch
ID possible opportunity	Determine market size, trends & use patterns to define targets	Design and produce prototype	Ensure prototype can be mass-produced	Identify test markets and begin end-user tests	Expand market availability or introduce nationally
Determine strategic fit to biz model	Test user attitudes & ID competitive advantages	Design packaging	Begin limited production in test runs	Solidify distribution channels	Monitor results and market response
Determine ways to differentiate the product	Define manufacturing requirements	Develop initial marketing/sales plan including naming & distribution	Confirm supplier commitments	Execute marketing/sales plan	Adjust operations, logistics and promo activities accordingly
Define criteria for success	Establish investment requirements and pricing, profitability & scalability	Fine-tune P/L model	Finalize marketing/sales plan, including packaging & pricing	Notify and equip Customer Service reps	
	Review outside factors (regulatory, political, etc.)		Fine-tune operations & logistics	Evaluate ROI	
			Fine-tune P/L model	Adjust operations, logistics, pricing & promotional activities	
Marketing, R&D and Sales	Same plus CFO, Ops, Quality & Product Mgt	Same	Same plus CEO	Same plus Customer Service	Same

"Only time will tell whether this merger makes sense or not."

22

How to Avoid an M&A Hangover

Some leaders view acquisition as a strategy central to their company's growth, while other leaders view acquisition as a tool that enables them to implement their strategy.

Whether you view acquisition as a strategy or a tool, there's no debate that mergers and acquisitions must be handled carefully. Properly conceived and managed, a merger or acquisition can accelerate an organization's profitable growth and widen the gap between its competitors. But if bungled, they can destroy an organization's culture, reputation, and earning power.

Enron, Tyco, and WorldCom have become classic bad examples of companies that built their twenty-first-century strategies on the backs of mergers and acquisitions. When the acquisitions failed to yield their promised results, greed, fear, and fraud took over, ruining Enron, bankrupting WorldCom, and taking Tyco to the brink of disaster. The senior-most executives from these three companies now face various phases of criminal and civil litigation on allegations of negligence and fraud. Whatever the courts decide, there's no question these failed acquisitions have cost thousands of people their jobs and their investors and employees billions of dollars.

This is not to say that a company looking to grow via acquisitions is ineffective, much less criminal. When used to fill gaps or to complement a core competency, acquisitions can be a smart way to build market share. The Bank of America/FleetBoston Financial merger, a $48 billion transaction that proposes to create a financial services giant with $966 billion in assets, weds two organizations whose respective growth and success has been driven by the dozens of acquisitions each company has made over the years.[121] Dean Foods' 2003 acquisition of Horizon Organic fills a gap in the former company's dairy portfolio. Comcast's December 2001 announcement that it was acquiring AT&T's cable television properties capped a five-year run of successful acquisitions that had taken the company's market value from $21 billion to $70 billion.[122]

Acquisitions are nothing new. Charlemagne, considered one of the greatest medieval kings, embarked on what we might consider an acquisition spree, when in about 773 he led a series of fifty-three campaigns "designed to round out his empire by conquering and Christianizing Bavaria and Saxony, destroying the troublesome Avars [and] shielding Italy from the raiding sword."[123]

Strategic fit, integration, and implementation are the keys to any successful acquisition, as Charlemagne clearly understood and emphasized during the forty-seven years of his reign. "In truth," writes Will Durant in his *Story of Civilization*, Charlemagne "had always loved administration more than war, and had taken to the field to force some unity of government and faith upon a Western Europe torn for centuries past by conflicts of tribe and creed. He had now brought under his rule all the peoples between the Vistula and the Atlantic, between the Baltic and the Pyrenees, with nearly all of Italy and much of the Balkans." Charlemagne relied on assemblies where smaller groups of nobles or bishops suggested legislative initiatives. Charlemagne formed chapters of legislation, and at these meetings, reported Hincmar, archbishop of Reims at the time, "The King wished to know whether in any part or corner of the Kingdom the people were restless, and the cause thereof."[124] Charlemagne, in other words, knew that there was much more to an acquisition than simply forcing his laws, customs, and culture on his newly acquired subjects.

Incredibly, some modern-day Charlemagnes do not fully consider the impact of the non-financial, non-legal aspects of their acquisitions. Teams of lawyers, accountants, and bankers may spend hundreds of hours tightening the deal, yet many times, the factors some may call "soft" are the very ones that cause deals to fall apart and mergers to fail over the longer term.

For those exploring the possible acquisition of faltering companies, the due-diligence process is a time for putting both organizations—the acquirer and the target—under the microscope. More than half of all mergers either fail to meet the financial expectations outlined at the time of the transaction or fail outright. And studies show that about half of the executives in the company being acquired leave in the first year, while about three-quarters of them leave within three years.

Business leaders dreaming of solving growth problems or expanding market leadership with a stroke of a pen must resolve difficult issues before completing the transaction. The management teams of both companies need to ask and answer tough questions and agree to terms before a merger or acquisition moves forward. Here are five deceptively simple questions:

1. Is This Merger Consistent with Our Vision?

Mergers rightly excite leaders who look to improve profitability by cutting redundant costs and expanding marketplace penetration. Yet the highest value of any successful merger comes from the ability of two senior leaders who view the merger less as a combination of the present than as an opportunity to create the future. This is the idea behind the Bank of America/FleetBoston Financial merger, since Bank of America chief executive Ken Lewis "has spoken of making his bank more of a force in managing the investments of affluent Americans."[125]

Credit J.P. Morgan (the man, not the company) with the idea of judging acquisitions on their future earning power. In December, 1900, Morgan discovered that Andrew Carnegie planned to expand his steel operations into a market Morgan already dominated. Morgan grew concerned that overcapacity and confusion would disrupt his plans. Morgan asked Carnegie if he would sell and, after a time, Carnegie named his price: $480 million. Morgan immediately accepted, basing his judgment "on a premise that was revolutionary at the time: expected future cash flows. He reframed the question from 'What are Carnegie's steel assets worth now?' to 'What will they be worth in the future?'"[126] Ask yourself if the merger will help make you a market leader, or help you maintain your dominance as a leader. If the answer is "Yes," take the next step.

2. What ROI Should We Expect Post-Merger?

However you choose to measure the impact of the merger—increased market penetration, acquisition of key talent, technology or patents, reduced operating costs, creation of a new business model—make sure your reasons and your goals are clear and realistic. The HP-Compaq merger was one of the most controversial mergers ever, with Walter Hewitt, son of one of the founders, campaigning aggressively against it. Ironically, this campaign of opposition helped focus attention on the issues that would contribute to or detract from the merger's success, resulting in the development of detailed plans addressing products, people, and profitability. HP pledged that the merger, once completed, would help the company cut costs "by at least $3 billion annually by 2004" and eventually break even.[127] Chief Executive Carly Fiorina is making this merger a winner. Do your homework, then shoot straight on the facts, projections, and other operating realities.

3. How Will Our Stakeholders Respond?

While you can't—or at least, shouldn't—consult non-retained outsiders while a prospective deal is in the works, you would do well to think through how each of your constituencies will react to a merger. "We've walked away from companies with autocratic leaders because their employees wouldn't fit in with our team culture," says Ammar Hanafi of Cisco Systems. Cisco has completed more than three dozen acquisitions since its 1986 founding and has a team of staffers dedicated to examining the culture of targeted companies and helping integrate them into Cisco.[128] Washington Mutual has acquired nearly thirty financial services firms since 1987. "We know what the regulators are going to ask for, so we might as well give it to them right away," says a Washington Mutual executive.[129] Moreover, just as employees and regulators are important, "what you do with an acquisition depends on the channels and the products that you and the acquired company are in," says Allstate Chief Executive Ed Liddy, whose company made two acquisitions totaling $2.2 billion in 2000. "You can't try to slam every acquisition into one mold." In a market-driven economy, your acquisition must make as much sense to the people outside and inside your organization as it does to the executives doing the deal. "We communicate, communicate, communicate. We say the same thing over and over again to the acquired company, to ourselves, to Wall Street. That way," says Liddy, "a common understanding of what we're trying to do can emerge."[130]

4. What Must Be Spun Off, Sold, or Cut?

For the HP-Compaq merger, senior leaders adopted an "adopt-and-go plan" in which competing HP and Compaq products were evaluated on their merits with the weaker of the two being scrapped. The initial goal was to reduce the product portfolio from eighty-five thousand to sixty-two thousand.[131] If you find yourself cutting more people, products, and services than you expect, you'd better take another look at why you think the deal makes sense in the first place.

5. Are Lines of Authority and Responsibility Clear?

The operational structure of the new entity must be clear and agreed on sooner rather than later if the merger is going to move forward and prove successful. Structure, roles, and retention become key issues, and while most large companies assemble integration teams to address these issues, it can be helpful to call in third parties to help with this process. "It's extremely important to reach out to the second tier of management quickly," says Jan Leschly, who retired as chief executive of SmithKline Beecham in 2000 after leading several acquisitions, including its $180 billion deal with Glaxo. "We used a consulting company to evaluate all our managers in every single country [where we had redundant operations]. It was a tremendous morale boost [for the managers of the acquired company] who didn't feel they were just being slaughtered."[132]

●   ●   ●

As on any big decision, move carefully through the due-diligence phase, do your homework, and stay true to your culture and strategy. Unfavorable answers and irreconcilable differences on any of these five broad areas can doom a deal or lead to an M&A hangover of epic proportions once the deal is done.

Part 6

Leveraging Change in Times of Distress

"*What we didn't have but obviously needed was an alarmist.*"

23

Avoiding Bears
The Nine Warning Signs of Trouble

No leader knowingly walks into trouble, any more than he or she sets out to fail. Yet surprisingly often, business leaders disregard early warning signals that indicate their business is headed for trouble. William Snyder, whose firm Corporate Revitalization Partners specializes in helping distressed companies throughout the US regain their financial health, told me that by the time his firm is called in to help rescue a distressed company, there's usually about three weeks of operating cash left in the till.

It doesn't have to be that way. The warning signals are there. They can show up in good times or in bad times, but they are particularly prevalent in times of distress. Ignoring them can be fatal.

There's a parable about a hiker that offers a glimpse into the mindset of executives who slowly but surely move away from the proven path of performance and discount signs of approaching trouble. The hiker, the story goes, finds himself alone and lost in unfamiliar territory. The terrain is rugged, heavily wooded, and inhabited by wildlife, including bear. As the hiker journeys deeper into the forest with the goal of reaching a point where he can regain his bearings, he begins to see bear tracks. He keeps going. The hiker then notices claw marks on trees. Undaunted, he pushes ahead. Next he observes a growing number of bear droppings. Even that sign doesn't convince him to turn around and pursue another direction. Before he knows it, he's face to face with a bear and it's too late to run. He's dead.

Sadly, an executive often will only bring in outside consultants—turnaround experts, bankers, investors, CPAs, lawyers, and marketing strategists—at the last possible instant when he finds himself face-to-face with a bear. When that happens, the executive becomes the punch line to another bear story: "I don't need to outrun the bear," says one hiker to the other after spotting a charging bear. "I just need to outrun you." Perhaps the business is saved from the bear, but those who delayed taking action are usually among the dearly departed.

Making the right choices—difficult and painful though they may be—will help a company push through tough times to survive and, perhaps, to thrive. Likewise, shirking responsibility or exercising bad judgment will eventually catch up to a company and cause it to fail—or cost those at the top their jobs.

Can bad outcomes be prevented? Often they cannot. But many times they can. "All wise [leaders] must . . . cope not only with present troubles but also with ones likely to arise in the future," wrote Niccolo Machiavelli nearly five hundred years ago in *The Prince*. "If you wait for [trouble] to show itself," continues Machiavelli, "any medicine will be too late because the disease will have become incurable." Ben Rosen, former chairman of Compaq and a dean of the venture capital world, might not agree with Machiavelli that companies in the later stages of a decline are doomed to death, but Rosen does believe that turnarounds are more difficult to implement than start-ups.[133]

Here's our list of the nine warning signs of trouble along with our perspective on the five phases of a turnaround situation. Finally, we'll show you how to create a "dancing recipe." All these are intended to save you from fatal encounters with bears.

Nine Warning Signs of Trouble

1. Disagreement among Leaders on Business Strategy

If you don't know or can't agree on who you are as a company, you will flounder. A tight strategy provides focus, which drives execution, which propels success. Most companies can only do one thing really well. Diversification and multi-pronged strategies can be effective if you're a giant company, but too much diversification can kill small companies and even a few big ones. If leaders aren't aligned behind a focused business strategy, don't expect your employees to be. And if employees aren't aligned, say goodbye to customers. You've got to agree on which customers make sense, which markets you will serve and, ultimately, which products and services that you're selling make money.

2. Peer Company Outperforming Your Company

Underperformance usually results from a bad market, a bad balance sheet, or bad management. It's hard to change a bad market—think airlines following September 11—though as we discussed in chapters 19, 20, and 21, there are steps you can take to push through one. But if you see that your competitors are doing appreciably better than you, then you're likely doing something wrong. "Most games," says legendary baseball coach Casey Stengel, "are lost, not won." Make sure you're taking care of the little things that add up to winning.

3. Inventory Backlog, New Orders Well below Forecast

As sales drop, inventories rise. So when your top line plummets and your margins begin to shrink because of lost customers or lost market share, your inventories will start stacking up. If you're selling widgets, watch your backlog. If you're providing services, watch the capacity of your people. Are you winning or losing a majority of your bids? Snyder says that too much of either one means your pricing is out of whack or, again, you're chasing your tail with a product or service nobody wants.

4. A/R Growing, Cash Flow Shrinking

Working capital gets squeezed as the amount of time to collect your bills lengthens, so you start stretching the payment you owe your suppliers. Declining cash may prompt an unplanned visit to the bank to attempt to borrow operating capital. Good luck.

5. Reducing Loss Reserves to Offset Lower Revenue

Changes in accounting policies, says Snyder, is another signal that a company is in trouble. Reducing your loss reserves because of lower revenue may help you prop up your company's profitability picture, but doing so simply camouflages the real problem and leaves your company even more vulnerable to unplanned and unforeseen events.

6. High Turnover, Low Morale, Pay Cuts

Like rats that know when to flee a sinking ship, workers can sense when a company is in trouble and will abandon it. It's an unfortunate, but nonetheless accurate, comparison. "When the market cycles down, revenues and profits are hit hard and in turn compensation is hit hard," says Trammell Crow Company chief executive Bob Sulentic. "The combination of these factors puts pressure on morale. We took early and aggressive action over the last two years to address the pending market downturn and an inflated cost structure. It was necessary but hard on our people. It impacted their morale and took some of the focus off customer service. There is absolutely no doubt in my mind that by the fourth quarter of [2002], our people had absorbed the changes, morale was on the way up, and focus had again turned . . . toward our customers."[134] Nobody said it would be easy, but taking the right action and taking it early is one of the first steps toward turning around a difficult situation.

7. Phone Calls to Customers Not Returned

The only thing worse than customers not returning your calls is an increase in calls from customers ringing you up to complain. The need to simplify and enrich the customer experience remains stronger than ever. Going a step further, knowing your customers' customers can help you predict and respond better to market trends. Your organization must know what customers want and take care of them. If you don't, your customers will go elsewhere.

8. Inability/Unwillingness to Focus on Key Problems

Your company will die if you fail to solve the right problem, repeat the same mistakes, or continue to reinvent the wheel. All three can waste time, money, and energy. As the earlier quote from Machiavelli argues, failure to correct these issues is demoralizing in the short term and deadly in the long term. Sometimes the answer to a problem comes from discovering you're looking under the wrong stone. A Fortune 500 company determined that competitive pressures would force it to close its Texas plant—one of twelve in the U.S.—and move operations to Mexico. The decision would cost the company millions of dollars and affect nearly four hundred workers. The good news is that this was the wrong problem. Before moving forward with the closure, the company retained our firm, and we conducted our own analysis and raised several pointed questions with management. The answers help illuminate a better solution, and happily, management was more than willing to change its decision. As a result, the company achieved better short- and long-term outcomes: it closed a plant with higher operating costs than the Texas plant, it initiated a program to lower operating costs in each plant by renegotiating economic incentives, and the Texas workers kept their jobs. The lesson: make sure you're aiming at the right target before you pull the trigger.

9. Payments Delayed/Missed, Bankers Are Nervous

The downward spiral continues when loans, covenants, and obligations to your borrowers are not met and go into default. Bankers and investors become increasingly nervous that real trouble is closing in. By the time this happens, you are well on your way to losing control of your own destiny because next they will call in someone else to fix the problem you failed to solve.

Five Phases of a Troubled Company

1. Denial

Like the hiker who ignored the signs that a bear was present, ignoring the nine warning signs of a troubled company is the first in a series of five phases of a company in distress. Failure to admit and address significant but isolated problems becomes costly. When warning signs indicate the company is or soon will be in a turnaround mode, management's denial of the situation heightens the problem and places an extra burden on the business and all its stakeholders. Unfortunately, studies show that turnaroud professionals are called in during the late stages of decline about 62 percent of the time.[135] Denial doesn't change reality.

2. Facing the Problem

Once management admits there are problems, executives decide either to take or to postpone action. When they postpone, it's usually because of one of three factors:

- Ego: recognizes the problem but perceives admitting the problem to others or bringing in outside help as a sign of weakness
- Paralysis: recognition that something must be done but an uncertainty of what action to take or an unwillingness to take it
- A wait-and-see attitude: a false belief that the existing plan will eventually produce the desired results, even though it hasn't done so yet

3. Taking the Wrong Action

Usually, the existing management team acts on the wrong things. Cuts are often necessary and can be effective, but only after identifying the right problem. Bad cuts are worse than none at all. Conversely, Snyder notes that "management many times will rely on more capital rather than making tough choices."

4. Change the Game

Assuming the company has survived the first three phases, it finally faces its problems. To effect change, the new plan must be different and must leverage the company's strengths. Reexamine the competitive landscape and rethink the business strategy based on the company's position in the marketplace. Isolate competitive advantage and areas where the greatest value is provided. Examine all assets (plants, products, programs, people). Determine what you'll operate yourself versus outsource to others who can provide products and services more efficiently. Examine all financials (loans, payables, A/Rs, forecasts). Test your new strategy through benchmarks and quick-strike research. Commit the plan to writing with milestones.

5. Implementation

Time is now of the essence. The difference between failure and survival is usually a matter of weeks. Management must shed unprofitable operations, drive core competencies, and meet schedules, deadlines and other commitments. A great strategy without the ability to execute it is just another opinion.

● ● ●

So be careful when you hit a rough patch of territory. There are bears out there.

The "Dancing Recipe"

On the following page is a simple but effective approach for solving problems that consultant John Dealey has shared with me and that we've used with our clients and among colleagues. Dealey often refers to this process as a "dancing recipe" because the data dances back and forth until a possible solution emerges.

Don't let the simplicity of this process fool you into underestimating its power.

Date_____

First, establish in your mind the current situation.
Next, determine how many problems are contributing to this situation.

+--+
| |
| |
| |
| |
+--+

List all of the problems in the box below.
Now take one problem and work through the process.

+--+
| What is the problem? |
| |
| |
+--+

+--+
| What caused the problem? |
| |
| |
+--+

+--+
| What are the possible solutions? (There must be at least 3, and we |
| believe that creative problem solving doesn't begin until you have listed |
| at least 10 possible solutions.) |
| |
| 1 .   6. |
| |
| 2.   7. |
| |
| 3.   8. |
| |
| 4.   9. |
| |
| 5.   10. |
+--+

+--+
| Which solution do you recommend? |
| |
+--+

+--+
| If the recommendation you selected were approved now, what could |
| most likely go wrong? |
| |
+--+

Revise your recommended alternative as needed and take action now.
Make it a habit not to leave what Dealey calls the "scene of the decision"
without taking some action toward the resolution you identified—even if
the action taken is an initial, small step.

"It's a game of power, speed, agility, and grace, but,
most of all, Tom, it's a game of points."

24

The X's and O's of a Turnaround

Sports is often a metaphor for business. So when is business a metaphor for sports? When the topic is turnarounds.

Oakland Raiders owner Al Davis hired outsiders in 1998 to take the Raiders back to the Super Bowl, and four years later they played in the championship game. In 2001, Tampa Bay Buccaneers owner Malcolm Glazer hired Jon Gruden, who capped an eight-year process of pursuing a Super Bowl appearance by winning it all.

The Dallas Cowboys are now moving forward again under new coach Bill Parcells. It's too early to pronounce the Cowboys perennial winners. But a 2004 *Sports Illustrated* poll shows that the Cowboys are America's favorite pro football team and third favorite professional sports team.[136] So it's instructive to examine the business factors that prompted owner Jerry Jones to fire Dave Campo and bring in an experienced turnaround pro to fix the problems. What did Parcells find when he arrived as the new sheriff at Valley Ranch? What steps did he take first? What must Parcells do to make the Cowboys a Super Bowl contender?

Pain Drives Change

As we observed in the previous chapter, a progression of events in any business points to increasing trouble.

Trouble starts with the loss of competitive advantage: in the Cowboys' case, three consecutive 5–11 seasons. It moves to worsening financial results—difficulty selling tickets and suites—and advances to additional financial pressure: the loss of prime-time TV revenue. Ultimately, sustained trouble leads to the realization that drastic action must occur in order to relieve the pain of losing—games, money, and stature. As much as he wanted to win again, it was this pain that drove Jones to do what many said he would never do: hire a strong-willed football coach.

There's no question Jerry Jones is the chief executive of the Dallas Cowboys. And now there's no question that Bill Parcells is the chief operating officer . The two men share a vision of winning, and winning big. Parcells's job is to execute on that shared vision, and he's using time-tested turnaround principles to make the Cowboys winners again.

Seven Principles of Successful Turnarounds

Jones brought Parcells into the Cowboys organization to change the game.

The deterioration that occurred before his arrival makes his job harder. Unfortunately, this is common among distressed companies. As we've already observed, few chief executives call early. So by the time turnaround pros are brought in, the need for change is urgent and, usually, drastic.

"When there's a coaching change," Parcells has said, "things change. Players change. Systems change. Philosophies change. Work habits change. The whole place changes."[137]

But even amid all this change, there are seven principles for engineering the successful turnaround of a troubled organization that never change. Bill Parcells is applying all of them. Here's his perspective thus far:

1. Establish Vision

Workers involved in a turnaround must know the goal. The Cowboys are a legendary franchise—one Parcells compared to celebrated teams like the Yankees and Celtics—with a commitment to winning. The vision is simple: Restore the team's winning ways and take the Cowboys back to the Super Bowl. "I'm looking for guys who are willing to do whatever it takes to win all the time," he says.[138] "I'm not coming back to coach practice."[139]

2. Be Honest

Never sugarcoat the facts in a turnaround. Parcells doesn't. "This [2003 season] is going to be a struggle," he says.[140] He made it clear he wanted players participating in his off-season program. "I want the team in condition. We've got guys I want to lose weight."[141] He made it clear that players that can't play injured won't make the team. "The late George Young had an expression that I remember well. He said, 'It's football season, and football players usually play football.' . . . When it's football season, whatever reason that comes up that's a deterrent to you playing is problematic."[142] Parcells also made it clear that players that can't perform will be cut. "Parcells is an honest man," says one player. "He tells you exactly what he wants, and then he expects you to do it."[143]

3. Set Clear Expectations

Whether you're losing games or market share, discipline (or the lack of it) is usually one reason why. It's been said Parcells's biggest mission is to change the Cowboys' recent culture of losing to one of winning. "You don't get medals for trying," he tells players, "you get medals for achievement."[144] He's posted signs in the locker room, saying "Prove you can win on the road," and "Dumb players do dumb things. Smart players very seldom do dumb things."[145] "You may think something's too simple," says one player, "but when you think about it, nobody has gone over this stuff in a long time. They just expected you to know it."[146]

4. Move Quickly and Boldly

A new leader's early actions are watched closely. For Parcells's first players-only meeting set for 1 PM, Parcells locked the doors at 12:55 PM.[147] The message was clear: You better think about overachieving in everything you do from now on. Later, a memo appeared on the Cowboys' team bulletin board covering rules and regulations. "Players' parking lot: Each car will be towed if not parked correctly. All cell phones must be turned off when entering the locker room area. No outsiders in the locker room area at any time. Update your address and telephone (must be able to be contacted—24 hours). NO FOOD In the locker room. Meeting rooms. Training room. Weight room." Parcells wants players taking a workmanlike approach to their careers.[148]

5. Construct Realistic Strategies

Faced with meager talent and salary-cap limitations, Parcells instructed his offensive coordinator to design plays that give his players an advantage by creating confusion and mismatches. He wants a grind-it-out running game to control the game's tempo, a defense that can keep games close in the fourth quarter, and enhanced performance from special teams. "I've always believed that if you want to improve your team, special teams are the quickest way to do it."[149]

6. Reorganize People and Reallocate Assets

Superstar Emmitt Smith is gone, taking with him his all-time NFL rushing title and hefty salary. Many other players unwilling or unable to meet Parcells's expectations have been cut. "We've all had players, if you've been in this league for any time, that they're not going to go where you hoped they would," says Parcells. "When you get to that point, it's a waste of everybody's time to continue the relationship."[150] Of fifteen coaches, only five from the Campo era have been retained by Parcells. Smart draft picks have enabled rookies to start and make an impact. The addition of proven veterans through free agency has shored up other weak spots. And smart preparation—particularly repeated drilling on game-day scenarios with zero tolerance for mistakes—has started to improve execution.

7. Focus Everything on Winning

In business, it's pleasing customers. In football, pleasing customers (fans) means winning games. "There are a lot of ways to win," says Parcells. "Your team has to understand that the opportunity to win a game is always going to present itself during the course of a game. What separates the teams that know how to win from the ones that don't is the ability to recognize that opportunity."[151]

• • •

"It's always the same for me," says Parcells. "You try to get good players. You try to get them into good shape. Then you try to put them into position where they can have the best chance to be successful."[152]

After just one season, the turnaround effect of Parcells is showing up in more places than the win column. For the 2003 season, Parcells's first, the Cowboys sold 511,224 tickets to its eight home games, and filled the stadium to 97.5 percent of its capacity—up from attendance during the 2002 season and well ahead of the league average of 94.9 percent capacity.[153]

Thanks to Parcells, and a 10-6 finish for the 2003 season, expectations are high for the 2004 season.

Implementing these seven principles successfully produces extreme feelings of satisfaction and happiness among turnaround professionals. It's why many are in the business. It's no different for Bill Parcells. "My happiness is for other people," he says. "It's not for my own ego or satisfaction. It really isn't. That's what you remember about football. All the big games I've been fortunate enough to be in, I just remember the smiles on those faces of the players."[154]

The fundamentals of a turnaround—whether you're leading a company, a college, a church or a sports club—never change.

"Those aren't buzzards, are they?"

25

Leading in a Down Economy
A Tale of Two Strategies

What does it take to face the challenges of a down economy? In such times, some organizations experience increased opportunities, such as the do-it-yourself housing and automotive after-market businesses. While consolidation and regulation are always threats, companies providing food, alcohol, tobacco, medicine, and small-ticket household items tend to be a bit more insulated from the slowdowns in consumer purchasing. But market uncertainty adversely affects most businesses.

There are proven strategies for finding new ways to wring costs out of operations and for jump-starting mature businesses. To lead successfully in a down economy, consider two strategies that represent different sides of the same coin: One strategy looks, questions, and cuts; the second looks, questions, and reinvests.

Both strategies depend on timely and accurate performance data. Leaders must pursue the truth and risk looking foolish for challenging conventional wisdom.

When Elizabeth became queen of England in 1558, her country's economy was at risk. Coins minted under the reign of her predecessors were becoming worth less than their face value, causing traders in foreign lands to demand gold or silver—not British coinage—from English merchants. This development threatened international trade because a gold and silver shortage created exchange problems. Inflation problems

211

hovered. Like those who had come before her, Elizabeth developed a plan to address this problem. But unlike her predecessors, she steeled herself to take and sustain the steps necessary to see her strategy through to its successful completion. She recalled all of England's coinage and revalued the country's money supply "without creating a panic, without disrupting trade, and without triggering a calamitous crisis of economic confidence."[155] The revaluation boosted English trade as credit abroad increased, expanded England's economy and helped make Britain one of the wealthiest European nations.

To survive the threats posed by her down economy, Elizabeth chose a bold strategy of change and reinvestment. We'll look at five other strategies for riding out—or even capitalizing on—a slumping market in just a minute. But first, let's examine areas where making cuts and adjustments can help.

Making Cuts and Adjustments

In the good times of economic growth, Tatum's Dan Jones says, businesses often become lax on expense controls. A down economy demands that leaders look critically and move quickly to make adjustments in ten areas where expense reduction can mean the difference between surviving and dying:

1. Authority to Commit

Implement specific, detailed, and written procedures, including purchase orders. Eliminate verbal approvals. Revise budgets. Hold those with budget responsibility accountable for sticking to them. Elizabeth might have said, "Off with their heads" if they failed to perform.

2. Purchasing and Receivables

Consider renegotiating with major suppliers, including pursuing discounts. Review collection procedures. "Cash *is* king," says Jones. "So monitor spending closely, deposit overnight cash and consider more aggressive collections to maximize cash on hand."

3. Material Costs and Inventory

Control material use and examine ways to improve operating cycle time. On the balance sheet, reduce inventory levels to match reduced raw material use. Consider eliminating low volume lines and eliminate unprofitable products and services. We'll revisit the benefits of focus below.

4. Freight and Facility Costs

Examine opportunities for suppliers and customers to bear shipping costs, and use standard rather than priority delivery for nonessential shipping. Consolidate and close sites, sublease excess space, or relocate to less expensive space.

5. Personnel, Payroll and Benefits

Review needs and adjust the workforce accordingly. Consider salary deferments for highly paid employees, furloughs for others, and delayed reviews and bonus programs. Implement hiring controls if they're not in place. Look for ways to increase employee contributions on benefits.

6. Travel and Entertainment

Reduce these expenses to the bare essentials and make sure corporate credit cards are monitored and controlled.

7. Utility and Telephone

Restrict LD access with security codes, and review fixed costs (phone and data lines) and cell and pager use.

8. Taxes and Audit Fees

Examine opportunities to lower property values and minimize sales and franchise taxes. Use internal audits for schedule preparation.

9. Interest Expense

Renegotiate debt and refinance to lower interest rates. During a particularly difficult period at Continental, CFO Greg Brenneman laid out the company's situation to his bankers. He explained what he needed from them to help to renegotiate the company's debt. When the bankers balked, Brenneman got up to leave, saying, "This whole company's worth $175 million . . . and you guys are in the hock for $3 billion. This isn't my problem." The bankers saw

Brenneman's point and soon were working with him to renegotiate the debt and help keep the company alive.[156]

10. Consultants

Value the thinking of advisors, consultants, and confidants. Some
consultants are necessary, even essential. Some are not. You must
know the difference and act accordingly.

Profiting from Change

Savvy executives running tight ships in good times use opportunities created in a down economy to widen the gap between their
company and the competition. Leaders can build market share
through one of these six market-facing strategies:

1. Do the Right Thing

In chapter 5, we discussed the importance of understanding your
own beliefs and then articulating them to your organization.
Adhering to your beliefs guides your actions. Few companies have
found their beliefs tested as the makers of Tylenol did in response
to the poisoning scare of 1982. Johnson & Johnson, we know,
placed its customers' welfare above its own. The product recall,
initially viewed as the company's death knell, earned the trust of
customers and has since made Tylenol's market leadership position virtually impregnable. Conversely, the 2001 Firestone-Ford
tire recall quickly became a model of what not to do in an equally
difficult situation. Firestone blamed Ford for its tire problems. So
while Firestone succeeded in raising doubts about Ford, the company failed to restore confidence about the safety of its tires—
which is what really matters. What beliefs, we may ask, did
Firestone's leaders show us?

2. Become More Focused

Keep your best and lose the rest. A down market is a great time to
tighten your strategy. Spend more time getting and keeping
your best customers. Jettison customers outside your core competency or those that take lots of time, money, and energy to find

and retain but add little to your profitability. It's hard to do, but worth the short-term pain.

3. Leverage R&D

Look no farther than Apple to see a company that's withstood the technology meltdown by bringing new product after new product to market. It's a niche player with a $6 billion position that continues to outmaneuver giants with market share and market capitalization ten or twenty times that of Apple. Innovation, as we've noted previously, can become your secret weapon. So resist the urge to cut. Despite the technology meltdown of 2001, Texas Instruments committed to keep its R&D budget intact as it trimmed in other areas, including personnel. After a prolonged industry-wide sales slump that caused the company's stock price to vacillate, Chairman Tom Engibous and TI are poised to harvest the R&D fruits they planted years ago.[157] Companies that continue to look for new ways of creating value for their customers will reap rewards—even in down times.

4. Increase Customer Service

While you're resisting the urge to cut R&D, also resist the urge to cut prices. Instead, raise the level of customer service. Answer the phone quicker and friendlier. Guarantee same-day shipping no matter when an order is placed. Give your employees more latitude in solving customers' problems. Every business has a product or service that costs nothing (or next-to-nothing) that its customers and prospects consider valuable. Find yours. Retailer Nordstrom is organized as an inverted pyramid that recognizes the fact that sales associates are the organization's closet link to its customers. All functions of Nordstrom are organized to support the sales staff. "The only thing we have going for us is the way we take care of our customers," said Ray Johnson, former cochairman, "and the people who take care of the customers are on the floor."[158] When you acknowledge that customers drive your business and not the other way around, you can keep bureaucratic red tape to a minimum, keep your workforce focused and motivated, and keep your customers happy and coming back for more—even in tough times.

5. Make Smart Acquisitions

See chapter 22. As noted there, successful mergers are driven by getting the right answers to questions in five key areas. Occasionally, two businesses in equally tough spots can join forces and succeed. Lockheed and Martin Marietta heard government officials summarize the post-Cold War environment by saying, "We expect defense companies to go out of business, and we will stand by and let that happen." Faced with three choices—fold, move to new markets, or increase market share in existing markets—the chief executives of these two businesses got their respective houses in order and then, in the words of Martin Marietta's Norm Augustine, set about making "the unlikely commonplace and the unthinkable almost inevitable."[159] Borrowing an approach from the Japanese semiconductor industry, both companies began searching for partners, "with each resolving to treat any consolidation as a combination of organizations." In 1995, Lockheed and Martin Marietta joined forces in a merger of equals. The company survived as the defense industry shrunk by 50 percent, and reshaped an industry in the process.[160]

6. Reinvent Yourself

Take a fresh look at how you stack up against your competition and what your best customers are buying. Trammell Crow Company built a real estate empire over forty years, but by 1989 carried significant debt and faced a saturated market. Two years later, recession gripped the country and commercial construction spending dried up. Under the leadership of Chief Executive Don Williams, the company took a long-term approach, assured that construction would rebound. But something had to be done immediately. Williams moved the company out of owning the buildings it developed and redirected the company's resources toward becoming a full-service provider that offered management, retail, brokerage and development. Partners left. Many sued. The change, while painful, repositioned the company, solidified its leadership position, and ultimately reshaped the industry. Today, chief executive Bob Sulentic is leading the company to capitalize on new marketplace dynamics, and under his leadership revenues have more than doubled over five years.

● ● ●

Whether you confront a down economy by cutting expenses or by capitalizing on the opportunities presented by change, avoid halfway measures and commit yourself fully to the actions you are directing. "No will in me can lack, neither do I trust shall there lack any power," said England's Virgin Queen. "And persuade yourselves that for the safety and quietness of you all that I will not spare if need be to spend my blood." In other words, give it your best shot.

Elizabeth's commitment to do her best to address challenges is what your team so desperately desires from you in times of change, uncertainty and difficulty. Do not disappoint them.

"No comment."

26

Leading in Times of Crisis

I t is a dreaded certainty that nearly every organization will eventually face a crisis that will threaten its reputation and customer base, if not its very existence.

Whether brought about by external forces or internal neglect, most leaders will find themselves fighting to manage their way through a crisis that will test their mettle under pressures few normal business situations ever produce. Your crisis may come in the form of layoffs, litigation, or loss of life.

The good news is that as the leader of your organization you possess the power to choose how to position yourself and your organization to respond to a crisis. Will you be ready to act or will you be left struggling as the situation drags you toward the abyss? For companies in transition—especially those facing a crisis—it's a stressful time. Your stakeholders—employees, customers, lenders, suppliers, partners, investors, regulators, legislators, and others—want to know what's happening, the plan going forward, and how they'll be affected. It's your job to tell them. So as you formulate and implement a plan to respond to the crisis you face, you will begin to understand why the Chinese words for "crisis" and "opportunity" contain the same character.

The stakes are at their highest levels for the rulers of a nation. Collapse of a country. Widespread economic depression. Famine. Plague. War.

When a brutal, premeditated and unprovoked attack on the United States by foreigners claimed the lives of innocent

Americans, the eyes of the nation looked to its top elected leader for an explanation and a response. The army was mobilized, a military initiative was organized, and thousands of infantry and specialists were dispatched to hunt down the perpetrators on their home turf. The year was 1916. Pancho Villa's raid on Columbus, New Mexico, resulted in the deaths of seventeen Americans, prompting President Woodrow Wilson to order General John "Black Jack" Pershing to pursue Villa across the US border into Mexico and bring him back dead or alive. Pershing stationed 150,000 soldiers along the border, the largest mobilization of troops since the Civil War, and what historian Louis Ray Sadler characterizes as "the last great cavalry operation in the United States Army."[161] Though Villa was never captured, Pershing declared his eleven-month expedition a victory, and Villa surrendered in 1920.

President Roosevelt faced a similar situation with Pearl Harbor. President Bush faced it with the terrorist attacks of September 11.

Few business leaders will ever need to tackle issues as weighty as those pertaining to national security. But the consequences of your words and actions in times of trouble, as we have already shown, can cause huge fluctuations in your company's market capitalization, change lives, and reverberate in countless other ways for years to come. A timely, comprehensive approach to trouble that displays candor, concern, and decisiveness can actually enhance your organization's reputation.

High-profile events exacerbate the risk of a damaged reputation because they likely will draw media attention—and attorneys. Such crises can include:

- Fatalities
- Product tampering and recalls
- Distressed financial situations and bankruptcies
- Labor conflicts, including strikes, closures and reductions in force (RIFs)
- Legislative and regulatory inquiries and investigations
- Environmental matters

- Hostile takeovers and shareholder suits
- Unethical behavior (i.e., fraud, discrimination, sexual harassment, etc.)
- Acts of nature (i.e., floods, fires, earthquakes, etc.)

Speak Out

Because these crises—with the possible exception of acts of nature—frequently will lead to litigation, you and your lawyers must decide quickly how you will address these developments. As we observed in chapter 17, saying and doing nothing in such situations is rarely an option, and the best attorneys know this to be true. The "no comment" approach is based on two fallacies. The first is that limiting advocacy to the courtroom will enhance the likelihood of a legal victory many months (or even years) from the time of the crisis. Failure to engage in a discussion of the issues outside the courtroom leaves your organization vulnerable to absorbing the impact of the internal rumor mill and outside negative publicity while waiting for the truth to emerge through the legal system. The second fallacy is that the legal victory—assuming there is one—will eventually vindicate the organization and its reputation.

Findings from consumer surveys are troubling: 38 percent of Americans believe a large company accused of wrongdoing in a lawsuit is likely guilty; 44 percent assume guilt when a government or regulatory agency is involved; and 58 percent believe a company is guilty when it responds with a "no comment" to charges of wrongdoing.[162]

Consider this scenario. A litigation matter is announced to the public, the company responds with a "no comment" and immediately six of every ten Americans believe that the company is guilty of the allegations brought against it. That's six of every ten potential jurors who one day may sit in judgment of the company. As a practical matter, that's also six of every ten employees, customers, lenders, shareholders, legislators, regulators, and suppliers. Thus organizations can suffer the most harm from crises in the court of public opinion. They can eventually win lawsuits, and liability insurance can pick up most, if not all, of the costs. A loss in the court of public opinion, however, can have a crippling long-term effect on an organization's reputation and, ultimately, its financial performance. As we observed earlier, Martha Stewart is the poster woman for this unfortunate truth.

Your response to a crisis can change public opinion, which affects behavior and, ultimately, the bottom line. Therefore, as a leader, you must address the issues head-on.

Prepare for Crisis

After making the decision that you will speak out on critical issues facing your organization, the next step is to prepare for a possible crisis. But how do you prepare for the unwanted? Effective crisis planning first involves a realistic and thorough assessment of key areas of organizational and product or service vulnerability. The objective is simple: By identifying potential problems, the organization can then act to remedy them now rather than having them flare up unexpectedly later. Can you and your organization ever identify every potential problem or plan for every contingency? Clearly not. But you can prepare your organization to survive even the worst crisis by eliminating as many areas of concern as possible and then creating a comprehensive and workable process for managing those that you haven't specifically identified.

When trouble looms or a crisis hits, the precise nature of your response will depend on the matter at hand. Jack Stone is a principal in Glass & Associates, Inc., an international turnaround firm, and has been working with troubled companies since 1970. He'll be the first to say that while each engagement is different, he agrees with me that you can nevertheless be guided by these seven proven steps, several of which should by now seem familiar.

1. Get the Facts

We've repeatedly emphasized the importance of gathering sound data. This particularly applies to acute crisis situations. "A lie," Churchill once said, "gets halfway around the world before the truth has a chance to put on its pants." When trouble hits, you must preempt, minimize, or mitigate the rumors, innuendo and misinformation that will be swirling around the crisis with reliable information. In particularly difficult situations, seek an objective, calm, unemotional, and unbiased perspective of the crisis, either from a trustworthy board member or other outsider. Working together, you can determine the nature and magnitude of the problem and an appropriate response. Your analysis of the situation must be reasonably thorough and totally objective.

2. Acknowledge the Problem

Again, as we've observed, denial is deadly. As simple (and difficult) as this sounds, when trouble knocks on your door, you must answer. Fix what can be fixed immediately. Say what you know. Admit what you don't know. Do your best to provide information that places the crisis in a context. Crises involving loss of life are tragic and painful. Acknowledge the tragedy and demonstrate your concern for all those affected. If the fatality is the first and only one that's ever occurred in the history of your organization, note that fact as part of your response. You're not trying to diminish the loss of life in any way, but you are emphasizing that the tragedy is an isolated one (if it really is) and that the organization has a long track record of operating safely. As the leader, you have the responsibility to acknowledge the crisis publicly to demonstrate that you are concerned, involved, and directing your team's response.

3. Anticipate Scenarios

Outline as many scenarios as possible that may occur in the course of moving through your crisis. Understand and prepare for the implications surrounding each scenario. Set objectives, rank priorities, and agree on what's critical and what's not. These scenarios and "trigger events" may be within the company's control but are just as often outside it. They include:

- Layoffs, closures, and likely future actions affecting employees

- Impact to customers, vendors, and third-party partners
- Regulatory involvement
- Competitor response
- Wall Street or investor response
- Nature, timing, and scope of media scrutiny

For a crisis that turns into litigation, every new phase of litigation (filing of charges, discovery, trial, etc.) will serve as an opportunity for both the defense and the plaintiff because each new phase will present a trigger point for renewed interest, particularly from the news media. Forewarned is forearmed.

4. Establish Key Messages That Tell Your Story

Your side of the story must marshal the facts and shape them into a message that communicates effectively in and out of a courtroom, a boardroom, a bar room, a congressional hearing room. In 1763, Samuel Adams and his fellow revolutionaries began making a case for separation from Britain by developing a message built on the premise that "the bulk of mankind are more led by their senses than by their reason." They designed their message of "taxation without representation" to motivate a group of Americans who were, at best, indifferent and, at worst, opposed to the idea of independence. The British, by contrast, relied solely on legal and military pressures.[163] When developing your story, it's critical for you, your lawyers, your board, and PR pros to craft it collaboratively, to always tell the truth, and to agree on the core message.

When CoServ's expansion from an electric utility co-op into telecommunications was hit by the telecom meltdown, lender support faded and a $1.1 billion note was called. CoServ sought chapter 11 protection, but this threatened constituents' confidence in the immediate wake of Enron's collapse. One message that our firm helped develop explained that market conditions in the telecommunications industry had led forty-four other telecommunications companies across the US and in Texas to seek bankruptcy protection during 2001. Another message emphasized the commitment to maintaining high levels of service for CoServ's sixty-four thousand customers during the bankruptcy.

5. Communicate Consistently and Continually

Having crafted your message, communicate it to all of your company's constituents—not just the lawyers—to help them understand the issues related to the crisis. This is particularly important regarding the legal process of a bankruptcy. CoServ developed materials for fourteen separate constituencies. Furr's Restaurant Corporation, whose workforce included a significant number of Hispanic workers, prepared internal materials in English and Spanish during its bankruptcy. Designate roles and responsibilities, including identifying a single spokesperson. If you are the chief executive, then you're the likely candidate. But make sure you're prepared to anticipate a range of questions and are skilled at returning the focus of the questioning to your key messages. A crisis represents an opportunity for an organization to develop stronger relationships with those groups that are critical to its success—employees, suppliers, investors and even customers. Keeping these constituencies feeling informed, respected, and appreciated during the crisis can mean the difference between simply surviving the problem in the short term and actually growing stronger in the long term.

It's not enough to respond to a crisis with a flurry of announcements followed by silence. Companies should keep communication lines open and resist the urge to stop communicating. Never communicate trade secrets, but remember that someone else will fill the news vacuum if your company doesn't. Proactive communication demonstrates openness and progress so make sure people that should be kept informed are kept informed. Counter negative publicity and public concern, but avoid fights, as Will Rogers used to say, with people who buy their ink by the gallon and paper by the ton. You can reduce some of the anxiety related to the uncertainty of a crisis by sticking to facts, integrating these facts into key messages and staying "on message."

6. Know the Boundaries

Remember the stated objectives and priorities and know how hard to push if and when a confrontation escalates. It's smart to know at the outset of the proceedings what those writing the checks are willing to risk in order to win. Your company's culture will help guide these decisions when its survival or reputation is at stake. A large transportation company faced an unprecedented onslaught of scrutiny based on its operating policies and, at the same time, the potential loss of its major client. The allegations of impropriety coupled with the loss of this large client would have resulted in massive layoffs and internal restructuring. When we were retained to help address the issues, one of the first decisions made had to do with how aggressive we were willing to be to fight the charges, since an aggressive rebuttal risked escalating negative media reports, alienating clients, and creating panic among employees. Armed with "good facts" and guided by the conviction that a series of passive responses would leave the company dangling in the breeze, the decision was made to go on the offensive. Doing so helped neutralize the media, strengthened the company's relationships with key external stakeholders, and allowed the company to keep its employees informed, calm and productive during the crisis. The company preserved its reputation, and management was able to negotiate a new long-term contract with its major client. Leaders must know what they're willing to give up and what they're willing to risk in order to win during times of trouble.

7. Expect the Unexpected

Since 1907, the Boy Scout motto of "Be prepared" has served leaders well in and out of scouting. Prepare for the worst; determine in advance the roles of each senior leader in times of trouble; and make sure each person with responsibility knows how to reach the other leaders at home, when they travel, and during holidays. Always keep in mind the various scenarios you contemplated in phase 3 because there's usually a surprise or last minute development. Stay alert and be ready for surprises.

• • •

In a world of high-stakes change, the leader of every organization will eventually find himself or herself called upon to explain some aspect of the organization's conduct. And with countless surveys, polls, and studies consistently confirming the obvious—that damage to an organization's reputation will cause a decline in market value—smart leaders prepare themselves for such a day of reckoning.

Layoffs

The test for evaluating your performance is whether your decisions maximize shareholder value, or, for private companies, deliver a satisfactory return on investment. In a tough economy, maximizing shareholder value often leads to decisions to cut costs rather than invest in new growth. And because expenditures for employees are usually one of an organization's largest costs, significant workforce reductions have become common. US Department of Labor statistics confirm that more than 1.5 million Americans lost their jobs in the period 2001–2003. The average spell of unemployment has increased to the longest since 1994. And while this phenomenon shall one day pass, it's worth examining some of the key dos and don'ts associated with layoffs.

Because when large-scale layoffs occur, leaders have even more of a duty to approach them compassionately—and strategically. If the rationale for staffing cuts is to maximize shareholder value, then dismissing employees should be accomplished in a manner that acknowledges the value of the organization's reputation. An organization can preserve its reputation by developing and implementing a plan that goes well beyond providing appropriate assistance and support to the employees whose jobs are eliminated. This plan depends upon three important characteristics: it must be truthful, it relies heavily on communication, and it looks to the future. And just as a crisis can enhance your organization's reputation, a plan that addresses the issues of a reduction in force (RIF) can transform an enterprise.

Beyond providing assistance to employees who are losing their jobs, you must articulate a new goal, protect morale, and motivate the performance of the remaining employees. In other words, you must rally organizational support in the wake of workforce reductions. Our experience shows that successful transformation plans contain these six key components:

1. Secure the Commitment of Supervisors

The success or failure of any plan to revitalize a troubled organization turns on the willingness of supervisors to support the new direction. While C-level officers set the new strategy, they need the support of middle managers to implement the plan. These managers must be assessed to determine their commitment to the planned changes and their ability to help lead change. "When you bring 100 people into the room," says Glass & Associates' Stone, "and describe the situation and outline your plan, look for the ones whose heads are nodding in agreement." Real change will not occur until enough leaders are promoted or hired into key jobs to implement the plan.

2. Articulate Changes—Not Just the Vision

A smart plan is useless if its creators cannot explain it so that those who must implement it can understand it. It's imperative to articulate effectively the rationale behind the changes, where you believe the new direction will take the organization, the reward for supporting the changes, and your commitment to those values, policies, and practices that will not change.

3. Establish a Sense of Urgency

Part of gaining organizational commitment is establishing a sense of urgency. The workforce must appreciate that in times of trouble, every day counts. Paralysis is fatal; productivity is paramount.

4. Commit to Ongoing Communication

Rumor and innuendo will derail a plan for change. So communication with stakeholders must be constant, candid and two-way. Create or enhance processes to elicit feedback to monitor response to change. Provide an outlet for workers to speak freely. The three most important pieces of information people want when faced with a difficult situation—particularly a financial turnaround—are: 1) Is the company going to survive? 2) Do I still have my job? 3) What can I do to help solve the problem? You must answer those questions.

5. Empower Others

Renewal also requires removing obstacles. Whether the obstacle is organizational, compensation-related or an uncommitted supervisor, these hurdles must be removed. Often, communication and obstacle removal go hand in hand. Failure to remove barriers so employees can begin undertaking the hard work of moving forward demoralizes your workforce and also damages the credibility of the overall transformation. Having communicated your objectives, give remaining employees the authority to act.

6. Institutionalize Change

To achieve desired short-term outcomes and develop a platform for sustained success, people must see how new approaches have improved performance. Real change occurs over time. Doing what you said you would do and celebrating small victories creates momentum as the work toward achieving long-term results continues.

● ● ●

Leading change in troubled times will require you to step up, speak out, and secure support from key stakeholders for your position. It will require those you lead and work with to change their ways of thinking, their approach to execution, and their level of commitment for your organization to emerge from troubled times.

Above all, ask yourself what changes are required of you.

Part 7

Sustaining Positive Change

"Not much, what's new with you?"

27

Measuring Change
Just Do It

L
ife is hard. So said Buddha about five hundred years
before the birth of Christ, teaching that suffering was
the first of his "Four Noble Truths."

Twenty-five centuries later, a life of change to achieve continued—or higher—levels of success is still hard for business leaders. Yet we can reduce the process of attaining and sustaining positive change to four simple truths:

- A solid understanding of your situation
- Clear objectives and strategies
- Implementation with conviction
- Measurement

Because the first three components have been addressed in detail in other chapters, here we'll cover measurement.

You must measure the actions of your company and its employees. This discipline can mark the difference between good companies and great companies. Measurement is the process by which real change takes effect, reaches its full potential, and becomes institutionalized within an organization.

- Are we making less progress than we expected?
- Do countless strategy and financial meetings continue to litter your calendar without result?
- Are deadlines pushed back time and time again?
- Could your employees be better focused on the company's overall goals and objectives?

If you answered "yes" to any of these questions, you're not alone. Most companies have these problems occasionally, if not chronically. So how do you turn procrastination, conflicting priorities, or even ambiguity into timely, specific, sustainable results with the power to deliver bottom-line impact? You implement measurement that will:

- Bring clarity, documentation, deadlines, and accountability
- Help deliver customer satisfaction and career growth for employees year after year
- Help drive sustained profitability for your organization.

Measurement—rigorous measurement—is hardly a new concept. In 1809, German mathematician Johann Carl Friederich Gauss published a study that brought a new level of rigor to predicting and measuring the "normal distribution" of errors. Many trace the origins of modern measurement to Gauss, and we recognize one aspect of his measurement tool as the "bell curve" that plots the probable occurrence of variation of the desired outcome.

Building on this model, Motorola engineers in the mid-1980s coined the term Six Sigma to describe variations from the mean (i.e., three sigma—"sigma" being the Greek letter to designate standard deviation—on either side of the mean) where process improvement is required.

Larry Bossidy at Allied Signal and Jack Welch at GE popularized the process, using it as a lever to change the culture—not just the performance—of their respective organizations.

Six Sigma is a problem-solving method that brings together proven processes that have been around for decades. It is ideal for complex situations with many variables and where the elements of rigor and objectivity are essential to understanding the cause of and solution to your toughest systemic issues. Six Sigma (and other comparable processes) bring clarity and focus to an organization's operations by drilling down deep to get the right answer—not just any answer—to such questions as:

- Have you assigned tangible measures to your most intangible organizational goals?

- Are your improvement initiatives linked to your most strategic issues?
- Are you tracking results?
- Are you receiving the return on investment for your initiatives that you expect?

Be warned. Measurement tools—virtually any meaningful measurement tools—are rarely quick fixes. And they are not for the faint of heart. Implementing measurement systems requires patience, discipline, lots of communication and the willingness to change habits, customs, and expectations. But, as I have shown in other chapters, when properly approached and executed, a measurement system will help leaders:

- Identify areas of greatest value to your customer (and therefore to your organization)
- Set priorities to become more effective at delivering customer value effectively
- Codify objectives, processes, and timelines using a common management framework
- Minimize errors, variations and waste
- Increase speed, productivity, quality and profitability

A key component of the Six Sigma process is a performance-improvement framework known as D.M.A.I.C., for:

- Define—the phase where the purpose, scope, and outcome of the project to be undertaken is established
- Measure—the phase where current performance is quantified
- Analyze—the phase where root causes are identified and then confirmed with data
- Improve—the phase where variations and non-value-added steps are removed or reduced
- Control—the phase where procedures are codified and institutionalized to a set of specific standards

While most measurement initiatives begin by seeking ways to wring excess costs out of an organization, it's important to note that a good measurement system can also help you increase revenue by identifying (or confirming) and then producing more effectively what your customers say they want.

Having identified your organization's so-called "value drivers," eliminated non-essential steps, and undertaken new processes that capitalize on your learning, the trick is to track, record, and sustain results.

A variety of off-the-shelf technology tools can be customized to track performance, but any process—even if it's just using pen and paper—that effectively drives results and measures accountability will work. Bill Winsor, former president of Infomart, a pioneering organization in the technology marketplace, held staff meetings every Monday for his entire organization. Each week, every department head stood up and shared two charts with the entire organization showing *Performance on the top three priorities of the previous week* and *Areas of focus for the coming week*. Very simple. Very effective. The human application and peer pressure are, frankly, more important than whatever technology tool you may choose to apply to help you in this process. What's important is to stick with these processes to deliver sustained results.

Here are the six steps for implementing and measuring the kind of change that produces bottom-line impact:

1. Align Interests

Once you have established, written down, and communicated overall objectives, departments and business units should develop specific objectives that support those overall objectives. It follows that employees should next develop their performance objectives in direct support of their supervisor or team leader's goals, creating a cascading effect that reaches down to the lowest level of the organization. When Larry Wheeler was hired in 1997 to run Mrs Baird's Bakeries, sales were not the problem. Wheeler quickly implemented a series of controls, checks, and measures to fix things on the earnings side rather than the sales side of the $300 million operation. Our firm worked with Wheeler and his team on a variety of initiatives, including restructuring, rationalizing, and repositioning certain products within the company's overall portfolio. Wheeler's realignment of interests to maintain sales while improving profitability helped the company quadruple its operating profit before selling in 1998 to Grupo Bimbo, Mexico's largest food company. To sustain success, it's critical that everyone agrees on what projects to tackle, what resources to allocate to complete the projects, and how to measure performance.

2. Gain Individual Commitment

Having achieved alignment on performance objectives, obtain and document agreement by all parties that they have committed to take certain actions to achieve their respective objectives. Documentation establishes clear roles and responsibilities. If these are reviewed regularly, there should be no surprises. Remember Southwest Airlines' overarching goal? "To treat every customer as we want to be treated." Ginger Hardage, vice president of corporate communication, directs forty-five people who are responsible for all of the airline's communications externally as well as with the company's thirty-five thousand employees. Part of her job involves gaining individual commitment on personal performance objectives. At Southwest Airlines, Hardage told me, "We conduct annual written performance reviews with lots of coaching in between. We take a really hard look at the first six months of employment." Commitment counts because it's the contract established between a supervisor and employee.

3. Set Deadlines

Deadlines add another layer of commitment and accountability. Accountability is best achieved through regularly scheduled peer group status meetings. As a mid-level executive at Ford in the 1960s, Lee Iacocca applied the corporation's systematic quarterly reporting to his own business unit. This kept key people focused on their ninety-day objectives, which in turn enabled them to fulfill their dreams.[164] Just as Iacocca led by being mindful of deadlines, so does FedEx. Cindy Connor told me that each team leader determines whether to review objectives daily, weekly, or monthly. You'd expect a company built on the promise of delivering packages overnight to be deadline-driven. "To achieve great things," said legendary conductor-composer Leonard Bernstein, "two things are needed: A plan and not quite enough time." Setting and keeping deadlines helps turn dreams into realities.

4. Allow for Variances

Events sometimes interfere with internal deadlines. Arie de Geus, who held senior leadership positions with Royal Dutch/Shell from 1951 until 1989 reported that successful companies value people more than other assets. Performance should be measured, de Geus believes, by setting "wide performance targets, in terms of final outputs. Leave lots of room for people themselves to achieve that output. Go for effectiveness rather than efficiency . . . Count on your people to take care of efficiency—if you trust them, and they trust you."[165] When it's necessary to make an exception to a previously agreed commitment, record the exception and make it with the full knowledge and acceptance of the team or the supervisor. Don't, however, allow the exception to become the rule. Too many variances will kill the project or, worse, indicate to others that deadlines and commitments are negotiable or arbitrary. Balance your trust of the individual with your expectation that all commitments be met.

5. Share Your Work

The documentation you have developed over the course of the project, month, quarter, or year illustrates your success and can prompt discussions regarding value with internal and external clients as well as with employees. The most successful professional service firms do this regularly with their clients as a matter of course—both through formalized, written evaluations and through informal, ongoing conversations between leaders from the service firm and company leaders that are receiving the work product. Ideally, the areas for measurement would include, but are certainly not limited to:

- Assessing your company's understanding of your customers' or client's business
- Evaluation of your staff's skills, ability, accessibility, and collaboration

- Results of work performed
- Overall management of the relationship and the engagement

Take note of both strengths and weaknesses. Ultimately, you want to determine your client's satisfaction with the work that's been done, the likelihood of future assignments, and whether there's a willingness to provide references. A candid information exchange not only pinpoints problems but also can help identify new revenue opportunities. Sharing information creates the platform for a long, mutually beneficial relationship.

6. Establish Consequences

Most people want to do a good job because they experience a sense of accomplishment and pride in a job done well. Think about the rewards—usually more than money, though money is important—you will bestow in recognition of completing successfully a project, engagement, or year. Think also about how you will deal with those who consistently fail to perform as agreed. You must strip away excuses and deal with reality. How you handle both your stars and your laggards will be reflected in the respect your team pays you.

● ● ●

Following these guidelines will not guarantee that any changes you initiate will succeed in the short term or even over a sustained period. But doing so will improve your odds of success. Embracing a disciplined approach that rests on a foundation of clarity and is upheld by regular measurement increases significantly the likelihood of two important outcomes. First, shared expectations with customers will lead to a greater understanding of the value your team brings to their business. Second, satisfied employees with clearly established responsibilities will be more productive and, therefore, more valuable to the organization.

28

To Survive and Thrive, Remember Darwin's Law

When Charles Darwin's *The Origin of the Species* was first published on November 24, 1859, it caused an immediate sensation because of the controversial theories it introduced about evolution and the implications for creation.

Beyond its historical, scientific, and even religious significance, the lasting effect of Darwin's work—subtitled "By Means of Natural Selection or The Preservation of Favored Races in the Struggle for Life"—is its imprint on and relevance to business.

> It may metaphorically be said that natural selection is daily and hourly scrutinizing, throughout the world, the slightest variations; rejecting those that are bad, preserving and adding up all that are good; silently and insensibly working, *whenever and wherever opportunity offers* [Darwin's emphasis], at the improvement of each organic being in relation to its organic and inorganic conditions of life. We see nothing of these slow changes in progress, until the hand of time has marked the lapse of ages, and then so imperfect is our view into past geological ages, that we see only that the forms of life are now different from what they formerly were.

Darwin's theories of "natural selection" and "survival of the fittest" are manifestos for today's business leaders. The line that separates successful companies from those that habitually underperform or fail altogether is such a fine one that leaders, as Darwin suggests, may miss seeing it "until the hand of time reveals it." Yet that line—while fine—is nevertheless distinct, and usually unforgiving.

Leaders looking to lead during changing times will do well to be mindful of these final guidelines that take their cue from nature, and have been well deployed by those business leaders, generals, monarchs, and sports stars whom history has judged to be the best of the best.

1. Grow Where You're Planted

Organizations that withstand the forces of change are led by those who understand what their companies do best. Whether you call it focus, core competency, or addition by subtraction, successful leaders say they would rather be great at two or three things than mediocre at ten. The remarkable French restaurant Lutèce on New York's East Side has "played a crucial role in the culinary development of the United States almost from the moment it opened its doors in 1961."[166] But on the eve of its Valentine's Day 2004 closing, its owner (who had purchased the restaurant in 1994 from the founder) acknowledged that, "We probably made a wrong turn a couple of years ago when we decided to make this menu edgy and more modern."[167] It can be hard, as Darwin noted, to understand the gradual effects of a misguided decision until months or years later. But abandoning an organization's strength is almost always risky. Great leaders build on strengths and minimize weaknesses.

2. Develop a Fertile Environment

We all recognize an organization with a productive culture the minute we come into contact with it—it's vibrant, energetic, and eager to please. People speak their minds in a spirit of genuine concern. "The difference between mediocrity and greatness," said coach Vince Lombardi, "is the feeling [teammates] have for each other. If you're going to play together as a team, you've got to care for one another as a team. You've got to love each other. There's no room for prima donnas."[168] Cultures condoning fear, politics, or even meritocracy are cancerous. They're certainly not places where truth and new ideas flourish, much less careers. The Columbia Accident Investigation Board reported that NASA's "cultural traits and organizational practices detrimental to safety and reliability were allowed to develop."[169] Barriers, in-fighting, and overconfidence bred a culture at NASA that resulted in a spectacular tragedy. Culture counts.

3. Adapt to Changing Conditions

I'm not talking about changing your values or adopting the strategy of the month. I'm talking about organizations that keep looking at the world around them; that watch, listen, and learn from current and prospective customers in order to expand, improve, and innovate. These successful organizations do not change their principles, but they do change their practices. Think of banks broadening their service offerings to become all-purpose financial institutions. They've expanded their service offerings to move beyond lending to include wealth management, insurance, investment banking, and brokerage capabilities. They've expanded their hours and channels into ATMs, the Internet, even grocery stores. Organizations that wait too late to adapt are destined for extinction.

4. Carry Out a Natural Plan

After the objectives have been set, the strategies selected, and the team engaged, it all comes down to execution. Cliff Harris, a four-time All-Pro safety on the Dallas Cowboys Super- Bowl-winning teams, tells an insightful story about Coach Tom Landry's approach to winning football games. Harris, in his first season in 1970, had a larger-than-life vision of what it would be like to play for the legendary Coach Landry. Harris came to the pros from tiny Ouachita Baptist University and predicted that whatever his fired-up Arkansas football coach could do, Landry would be sure to top. So as Harris gathered with the other players before their first game that season, he expected Landry to deliver a pep talk like he'd never heard before. Landry stepped to the front of the room and said, "You're a great team. You've got a good game plan that you've studied. You've practiced hard. Let's go execute." That was it. No "Win-one-for-the-Gipper" speech. No yelling. No pep talk. No emotion. Rather, Landry conveyed the belief that "This is what you're paid to do," the realization that "I've helped you get prepared to do it," and the confidence that "you will be successful if you execute properly." There's no question that Tom Landry was an inspiration to his team and had other ways of motivating players. All great coaches and, for that matter, business leaders do. But Coach Landry believed that consistent execution ultimately wins football games.[170] So it is in life, business, and school. Perform or perish.

Brian Alford is the head of the Corporate Communications and Community Services department at OGE Energy Corp. in Oklahoma City. On the wall outside his office hangs a framed poster entitled "The Essence of Survival." It reads,

> *Every morning in Africa, a gazelle wakes up. It knows it must run faster than the fastest lion or it will be killed. Every morning, a lion wakes up. It knows it must run faster than the slowest gazelle or it will starve to death. It doesn't matter whether you are a lion or a gazelle . . . when the sun comes up, you'd better be running.*

Taking charge in changing times is a matter of survival.

From the pre-Cambrian swamps Darwin studied, to the battlefields of the world, to a business climate of change, confusion, and uncertainty, the maxims remain the same. Stay alive, adapt, and execute your new plan. Your responsibility as the leader of an organization caught up in changing times is to keep your organization alive through honest means, and to keep things moving forward.

If you remember nothing else, remember Darwin's view of success: "It is not the strongest of the species that survives, nor the most intelligent; it is the one that is most adaptable to change."

Acknowledgments

Churchill got it right when he said, "Writing a book is an adventure. To begin with, it is a toy and an amusement; then it becomes a mistress, and then it becomes a master, and then a tyrant. The last phase is that just as you are about to be reconciled to your servitude, you kill the monster, and fling him out to the public."

My own book adventure began when Patti Clapp asked me to expand an essay I'd written entitled "The Cost of Leadership" into a speech for the Greater Dallas Chamber of Commerce. Being a fan of Patti's and believing that transforming an essay into a speech an easy task, I readily agreed. But it took more work than I'd imagined and, once completed, prompted me to consider one more transformation. *Could this speech become a book?* I wondered. Ken Bradford had recently written and published a book on effective public speaking, and he became a source of advice and encouragement. So off I went.

My wife Janet read the first few chapters, and told me in her inimitable style that she just might be willing to buy and actually read a book like this. That's when the book became my master. Paige Dawson helped me in ways too numerous to name, and Rosanne Hart brought me together with my publisher, Jill Bertolet. Jill and her team at Tapestry Press took a chance on a first-time author, and I thank them for their confidence in me and all that they've done to make the book a reality. Paul Brassey edited the manuscript, bringing brevity, insight, and grace to the task. The team at Eisenberg & Associates, who designed our firm's logo in 1994, applied their brilliance to the book's cover design. And Bill Scott got everything to fit, which wasn't easy.

My profound thanks go to those who agreed to read the manuscript in its early stages and allow their good names to be associated with this work. And thanks go to the Bustin & Co. consultants who helped inform many of the positions shared in this book, and whose best work for our clients is illuminated here. You know who you are. The Rev. Thomas Q. Robbins provided insight and inspiration. Many friends and clients allowed me to share their experiences in this book, and though you are too numerous to name, I thank you one and all.

The biggest thanks are reserved for the leaders at organizations who entrust us with their hopes and fears and dreams and then allow us to work together to address them. It is my hope that the lessons we have learned together and that I have shared here will inspire the next generation of leaders to embrace change and harness its power.

Suggested Reading

The Art of the Long View by Peter Schwartz, Currency Doubleday, 1991.

The Autobiography of Benjamin Franklin, Barnes & Noble Books.

Built to Last by James Collins and Jerry Porras, Harper Business, 1994.

Comeback by Martin Puris, Random House, 1999.

Competitive Advantage by Michael E. Porter, Free Press, 1985.

Competitive Strategy by Michael E. Porter, Free Press, 1980.

The Discipline of Market Leaders by Michael Treacy and Fred Wiersema, Addison-Wesley, 1995.

Elizabeth I, CEO by Alan Axelrod, Prentice Hall Press, 2000.

Every Business Is a Growth Business by Ram Charan and Noel M. Tichy, Times Books, 1998.

Execution: The Discipline of Getting Things Done by Larry Bossidy and Ram Charan with Charles Burck, Crown Publishing Group, 2002.

The Fables of Aesop selected by David Levine, Dorset Press, 1975.

The Five Temptations of a CEO by Patrick Lencioni, Jossey-Bass, 1998.

The Great Game of Business by Jack Stack, Currency Doubleday, 1992.

How Great Generals Win by Bevin Alexander, Avon Books, 1993.

How to Win Friends & Influence People by Dale Carnegie, Simon and Schuster, 1936.

In Search of Excellence by Thomas J. Peters and Robert H. Waterman, Jr., Warner Books, 1984.

Managing for Results by Peter F. Drucker, Harper & Row Publishers, Inc., 1964.

Only the Paranoid Survive by Andy Grove, Doubleday, 1996.

Organizing Genius by Warren Bennis and Patricia Ward Biederman, Addison-Wesley, 1997.

Positioning: The Battle for Your Mind by Al Ries and Jack Trout, MacGraw-Hill, 2000.

The Prince by Niccolo Machiavelli, Penguin Classics.

The Screwtape Letters by C.S. Lewis, Harper Collins, 1942.

The 7 Habits of Highly Effective People by Stephen R. Covey, Simon & Schuster, 1989.

The Trusted Advisor by David Maister, Free Press, 2000.

Turning The Thing Around by Jimmy Johnson as told to Ed Hinton, Hyperion, 1993.

Notes

1   Anthony Bianco, "Talking to the Troops" from "The Warren Buffett You Don't Know," *Business Week*, July 5, 1999.

2   News release, "62 percent of Americans tell CEOs 'You are not doing enough to restore trust and confidence in America,'" Golin/Harris, July 24, 2002.

3   News release, "Fourth Annual Survey of Executives Shows Unethical Conduct, Bad Press Key Threats to Corporate Reputation," Harris Interactive, June 5, 2002.

4   Anthony Bianco, William Symonds and Nanette Byrnes, "The Rise and Fall of Dennis Kozlowski," *Business Week*, December 23, 2002.

5   Landon Thomas, "Officials in 2 States Urge Big Board Chief to Quit," *The New York Times*, September 17, 2003.

6   Ibid.

7   David F. Larcker, *Directorship*, Vol. XXVI No. 5, Wharton School of Business at the University of Pennsylvania, May 2000.

8   Louis Uchitelle, "Latest Style For Pruning Companies Lop the Top," *The New York Times*, June 18, 2000.

9   "CEO Job Security is Declining Throughout the World," Booz Allen Hamilton, June 17, 2002.

10   "2002 Route to the Top," *Chief Executive*/Spencer Stuart, February 2002.

11   "The Crisis of Confidence Hasn't Reached the Workplace," Gallup News Service, July 2, 2002.

12   News release, "Global Survey Shows CEOs Taking Greater Responsibility for Corporate Reputations," Hill and Knowlton, October 3, 2003.

13   Dawn Wotapka, "Mary Kay Consultants to paint the town pink," *The Dallas Morning News*, July 18, 2003.

14   William Safire and Leonard Safir, *Leadership*, Galahad Books, 2000.

15   Speech at the University of British Columbia "on the occasion of the special congregation," May 9, 1960.

16   David McCullough, *John Adams*, Simon & Schuster, 2001.

17   Thomas J. Watson, Jr., *A Business and Its Beliefs: The Ideas That Helped Build IBM*, McGraw-Hill, Inc., 1963.

18   Louis Lavelle, "What Campbell's New Chief Needs To Do Now," *Business Week*, June 25, 2001.

19   Colin Powell, "18 Lessons from a very successful leader," LittleAfrica.com.

20   William Safire and Leonard Safir, "Leadership," Galahad Books, 2000.

21   Angela Shah and Eric Torbenson, "'Truly dreadful' quarter for AMR," *The Dallas Morning News*, April 24, 2003.

22   Eric Torbenson, "Doubts grow about Carty," *The Dallas Morning News*, April 20, 2003.

23   Tyler Kepner, "Torre Forgets. Can He Forgive?," *The New York Times*, April 22, 2003.

24   Speech, "Creating a Culture That Lasts," at Dallas 100 Leadership Series, March 18, 2003.

25   Speech before the Canadian Senate and House of Commons, Ottawa, Canada, December 30, 1941.

26   Jay Greene, "Small biz: Microsoft's Next Big Thing?," Business Week, April 21, 2003.

27   Douglas Jehl, "Spokesman Molded by Urban Warfare," *The New York Times*, April 9, 2003.

28   Steve Lohr, "He Loves to Win. At I.B.M., He Did," *The New York Times*, March 10, 2002.

29   Ibid.

30   Ibid.

31   Ibid.

32   David McCullough, *John Adams*, Simon & Schuster, 2001.

33   Speech at Southern Methodist University's Dallas 100 reception for winning chief executives, October 4, 2001.

34   David Fraser, *Knight's Cross*, HarperCollins Publishers, 1993.

35   Wess Roberts, "Leadership Secrets of Attila The Hun," Warner Books, 1985.

36   Ibid.

37   William Safire and Leonard Safir, *Leadership*, Galahad Books, 2000.

38   Ibid.

39   Letter of Instruction to the Captains of the Virginia Regiments, July 29, 1759.

40 Mary Kay website.

41 Dawn Wotapka, "Mary Kay Consultants to paint the town pink," *The Dallas Morning News*, July 18, 2003.

42 Alan Axelrod, *Elizabeth I, CEO*, Prentice Hall Press, 2000.

43 William Safire and Leonard Safir, "Leadership," Galahad Books, 2000.

44 Transcript of interview on CNN's Cold War series, episode 10, "Cuba," November 29, 1998.

45 Daniel McGinn, "The CEO's Challenge," *Newsweek*, April 28, 2003.

46 Jimmy Johnson as told to Ed Hinton, *Turning The Thing Around: My Life in Football*, Hyperion, 1993.

47 Ibid.

48 Robert Slater, "Will the real John Chambers stand up?," news.com, February 4, 2003.

49 Andrew Park, "EDS: What Went Wrong," *Business Week*, April 7, 2003.

50 Al Kaltman, *Cigars, Whiskey & Winning*, Prentice Hall Press, 1998.

51 Speech, "Leadership Through the Years," at Dallas 100 Leadership Series, September 17, 2002.

52 Betsy Morris, "The Accidental CEO," Fortune, June 9, 2003.

53 Ibid.

54 Ibid.

55 Dr. Joyce Tyldesley, "The Private Lives of the Pyramid-Builders," BBCi, September 20, 2002.

56 Dr. Aidan Dodson, "The Great Pyramid: Gateway to Eternity," BBCi, September 16, 2002.

57 Ibid.

58 Dr. Joyce Tyldesley, "The Private Lives of the Pyramid-Builders," BBCi, September 20, 2002.

59 Ibid.

60 Dr. Joyce Tyldesley, "Development of Pyramids," BBCi, September 20, 2002.

61 Ibid.

62 Ibid.

63 John Baines, "The Story of the Nile," BBCi, September 20, 2002.

64 Bernard Ryan, Jr., "Advertising in a Recession," American Association of Advertising Agencies, 1999.

65 Speech, "Timeless Values: Gateway to the Future," at Ernst & Young-SMU Management Briefing Series, March 28, 2002.

66   Maria Halkias, "Refashioning a retailer," *The Dallas Morning News*, January 23, 2003.

67   John Markoff, "Apple Returns to Profitability on Strength of New Portable PC," *The New York Times*, April 19, 2001.

68   "Executives Report Competitive Intelligence Needs," Strategy Software, Inc. news release, April 9, 2001.

69   Gerry Khermouch, "The Best Global Brands," *Business Week*, August 5, 2002.

70   Ibid.

71   Andrew Ross Sorkin and David D. Kirkpatrick, "AOL Time Warner Drops 'AOL,'" *The New York Times*, September 19, 2003.

72   Ibid.

73   Associated Press, "Safeway CEO under pressure," *The Dallas Morning News*, January 31, 2004.

74   Kyle Nagel, "The philosophical cowboy," *The Dallas Morning News*, November 6, 2003.

75   Ibid.

76   Stephen R. Covey, *The 7 Habits of Highly Effective People*, Simon & Schuster, 1989.

77   Shelly Branch, "So Much Work, So Little Time," *Fortune*, February 3, 1997.

78   Jon Fine, "Top marketers desert Martha," *Advertising Age*, August 25, 2003.

79   Constance L. Hays, "Martha Stewart Magazine Cuts Ad Rate Base, as Readers Decline," *The New York Times*, October 10, 2003.

80   Constance L. Hays and Leslie Eaton, "Martha Stewart, Near Trial, Arranges Her Image," *The New York Times*, January 20, 2004.

81   Stephen R. Covey, *The 7 Habits of Highly Effective People*, Simon & Schuster, 1989.

82   Keith H. Hammonds, "Business Fights Back: Continental's Turnaround Pilot," *Fast Company*, December 2001.

83   David and Shirley Thielen, *The 12 Simple Secrets of Microsoft Management: How to Think and Act Like a Microsoft Manager and Take Your Company to the Top*, McGraw Hill, 1999.

84   "The Tulip Trade," from De Koning's *History of Haarlem*, 1635.

85   John Markoff, "Apple Returns to Profitability on Strength of New Portable PC," *The New York Times*, April 19, 2001.

86   Norm Brodsky, "Streets Smarts," *Inc.* magazine, July 1999.

87   Speech, "The More Things Change, The More Things Change," at Dallas 100 Leadership Series, September 3, 2003.

88   Ibid.

89   "Dallas 100 Winners, Multiple Years," Caruth Institute for Entre-preneurship, Cox School of Business, Southern Methodist Univer-sity, 2004.

90   "America's oldest family companies," *Family Business*, Autumn 2003.

91   Ibid.

92   Ibid.

93   Eric Hoffer, *Reflections on the Human Condition*, Harper Collins, 1973.

94   Noel M. Tichy and Stratford Sherman, *Control Your Destiny or Someone Else Will: How Jack Welch Is Turning General Electric into the World's Most Competitive Corporation*, Doubleday, 1992.

95   Speech, "Timeless Values: Gateway to the Future," at Ernst & Young-SMU Management Briefing Series, March 28, 2002.

96   Fred Vogelstein, "Mighty Amazon," Fortune, May 26, 2003.

97   Wendy Zellner with Michael Arndt, "Holding Steady: As rivals sputter, can Southwest stay on top?," *Business Week*, February 3, 2003.

98   Eric Torbenson, "Southwest adds 2 St. Louis flights," *The Dallas Morning News*, November 14, 2003.

99   Susan Greco, "Choose or Lose," *Inc.*, December 1998.

100 Andy Grove, *Only the Paranoid Survive*, Doubleday, 1996.

101 Brian Dumaine, "Times Are Good? Create A Crisis," *Fortune*, June 28, 1993.

102 Shawn Tully, "So Mr. Bossidy, We Know That You Can Cut, Now Show Us That You Can Grow," *Fortune*, August 21, 1997.

103 Speech at the University of Michigan Business School, Multi-Disci-plinary Action Project Kickoff, March 10, 1998.

104 Honeywell website.

105 David Greising, "I'd Like the World To Buy A Coke," *Business Week*, April 13, 1998.

106 Ram Charan and Noel M. Tichy, *Every Business Is a Growth Business*, Times Books, 1998.

107 Ibid.

108 Claudia H. Deutsch, "FedEx Moves to Expand With Purchase of Kinko's," *The New York Times*, December 31, 2003.

109 Ibid.

110 Speech at Petroleum Club, Burnt Orange Productions private reception, October 15, 2003.

111 Ibid.

112 Eric Harrison, "UT takes filmmaking to new level," *Houston Chronicle*, September 10, 2003.

113 Jean Froissart quoted by Winston Churchill, *History of the English Speaking Peoples*, Dorset Press, 1956.

114 Product Development Institute website.

115 "FedEx Corporate History" from FedEx website.

116 "Speed Based Development" speech at Product Development & Management Association (PDMA) Annual International Conference, October 7, 2003.

117 Ibid.

118 Sherri Day, "New Products Help PepsiCo To 13% Rise in Earnings," *The New York Times*, October 8, 2003.

119 David Barboza, "Can Kraft Trim the Fat in an Oreo World?," *The New York Times*, July 26, 2003.

120 Claudia H. Deutsch, "For Mighty Gillette, These Are the Faces of War," *The New York Times*, October 12, 2003.

121 Patrick McGeehan, *The New York Times*, October 28, 2003.

122 Stephanie N. Mehta, *Fortune*, July 21, 2003.

123 Will Durant, *Story of Civilization. The Age of Faith*, vol. 4, Simon & Schuster 1950.

124 Ibid.

125 Patrick McGeehan, *The New York Times*, October 28, 2003.

126 Ron Chernow, *The House of Morgan*, 1990.

127 Cliff Edwards with Andrew Park, "HP and Compaq: It's Showtime," *Business Week*, June 17, 2002.

128 Claudia H. Deutsch, "The Deal Is Done. The Work Begins," *The New York Times*, April 11, 1999.

129 George Anders, "Seven Lessons From WaMu's M&A Playbook," *Fast Company*, January 2002.

130 "A CEO Roundtable on Making Mergers Succeed," *Harvard Business Review*, May-June 2000.

131 Cliff Edwards with Andrew Park, "HP and Compaq: It's Showtime," *Business Week*, June 17, 2002.

132 Ibid.

133 Martin Puris, "A Riddle Wrapped In A Mystery Inside An Enigma," *Comeback*, Random House, 1999.

134 Robert E. Sulentic, Letter to shareholders, 2002 Trammell Crow Company annual report.

135 "Survey Says Growth in Turnaround Busniess May Be Leveling Off," Turnaround Management Association *Journal of Corporate Renewal*, September, 2003.

136 "Fans Speak: Cowboys Rule," *The Dallas Morning News*, July 9, 2004.

137 Tim Cowlishaw, "Parcells fits his assistants for muzzles," *The Dallas Morning News*, January 29, 2003.

138 Jean-Jacques Taylor, "Signs of the Times," *The Dallas Morning News*, May 18, 2003.

139 Jean-Jacques Taylor, "Juiced offense, new attitude have Cowboys making ascent," *The Dallas Morning News*, October 7, 2003.

140 Kevin Blackistone, "Parcells has no illusions for '03," *The Dallas Morning News*, August 4, 2003.

141 Rick Gosselin, "Parcells: Content just to coach," *The Dallas Morning News*, March 27, 2003.

142 Brian Davis, "Earning job can be a pain," *The Dallas Morning News*, August 7, 2002.

143 Jean-Jacques Taylor, "Signs of the Times," *The Dallas Morning News*, May 18, 2003.

144 Jean-Jacques Taylor, "Tackle rejoins Parcells," *The Dallas Morning News*, March 6, 2003.

145 Jean-Jacques Taylor, "Stopping bad habits cold," *The Dallas Morning News*, March 7, 2003

146 Juliet Macur, "Bill's world: chasing NFL immortality," *The Dallas Morning News*, June 8, 2003.

147 Frank Luksa, "Cowboys culture changes on Parcells' watch," *The Dallas Morning News*, March 15, 2003.

148 Juliet Macur, "Bill's world: chasing NFL immortality," *The Dallas Morning News*, June 8, 2003.

149 Jean-Jacques Taylor, "Master builder," *The Dallas Morning News*, August 21, 2003.

150 Todd Archer, "Cornerbacks may get playing time," *The Dallas Morning News*, December 4, 2003.

151 Jean-Jacques Taylor, "'Fear of failure' motivates Parcells," *The Dallas Morning News*, May 7, 2003.

152 Tim Cowlishaw, "Just remember: These things take time," *The Dallas Morning News*, August 21, 2003.

153 Katie Fairbank, "Game has gotten tougher for sports teams," *The Dallas Morning News*, March 14, 2004.

154 Todd Archer, "Parcells' passion bonds team," *The Dallas Morning News*, November 25, 2003.

155 Alan Axelrod, *Elizabeth I, CEO*, Prentice Hall Press, 2000.

156 Martin Puris, "Gordon Bethune: The Mechanic," *Comeback*, Random House, 1999.

157 Crayton Harrison, "Ready for the next phase," *The Dallas Morning News*, October 7, 2003.

158 Robert Spector, *The Nordstrom Way*, John Wiley & Sons, 1995.

159 Norman R. Augustine, "Reshaping an Industry: Lockheed Martin's Survival," Harvard Business School Press, 1997.

160 Ibid.

161 Rick Nathanson, "U.S. chased Villa into mythology, filmmaker says," *The Dallas Morning News*, November 27, 1993.

162 News release, "Hill and Knowlton Survey Shows Companies Under Scrutiny," Hill and Knowlton, July 23, 2002.

163 See Scott M. Cutlip, Allen H. Center, Glen M. Broom, *Effective Public Relations* (6th ed.), Prentice-Hall, 1985.

164 Lee Iacocca with William Novak, *Iacocca*, Bantam Books, 1984.

165 Arie de Geus, *The Living Company: Habits for Survival in a Turbulent Business Environment*," Harvard Business School Publishing, May 2002.

166 Eric Asimov, "C'est la Fin! Lutèce Closing After 43 Years," *The New York Times*, February 11, 2004.

167 Ibid.

168 Lee Iacocca with William Novak, *Iacocca*, Bantam Books, 1984.

169 "Excerpts From Report of the Columbia Accident Investigation Board," *The New York Times*, August 27, 2003.

170 Speech at Southern Methodist University's Dallas 100 reception for winning chief executives, October 14, 2003.

About the Author

GREG BUSTIN helps leaders capitalize on change. He has worked with executives—including the chief executives of many of America's most respected companies—in connection with new ventures, takeover attempts, bankruptcies, industry restructuring, and market entries. He has also directed the launches of more than a hundred new products and services. Bustin's advice on effective management has been published in *The Wall Street Journal*, *Financial Executive*, and *The Dallas Morning News*, among others. He also speaks frequently on business and leadership issues. He served as a national judge evaluating marketing excellence from 1987–2002. He founded Bustin & Co. in 1994 after serving as executive vice president of Edelman Worldwide and general manager of a division of what is now DDB Worldwide. Bustin is a graduate of The University of Texas at Austin, where he served as an Advisory Board member of the College of Communication from 1998 until 2004. Bustin is a board member of the Dallas chapter of the Turnaround Management Association, and since 1998 has been actively involved in Dallas 100, a program that recognizes fast-growing companies.

www.bustin.com.